TALES FROM THE DETROIT PISTONS

With Reflections of Rick Mahorn and Joe Dumars

PERRY A. FARRELL

www.SportsPublishingLLC.com

ISBN: 1-58261-778-3

Publishers: Peter L. Bannon and Joseph J. Bannon Sr.
Senior managing editor: Susan M. Moyer
Acquisitions editor: Dean Reinke
Developmental editor: Dean Miller
Art director: K. Jeffrey Higgerson
Dust jacket design: Joseph T. Brumleve
Project manager: Alicia Wentworth and Kathryn R. Holleman
Imaging: Heidi Norsen and Kerri Baker
Copy editor: Cynthia L. McNew
Photo editor: Erin Linden-Levy
Vice president of sales and marketing: Kevin King
Media and promotions managers: Cory Whitt (regional),
    Randy Fouts (national), Maurey Williamson (print)

Printed in the United States of America

Sports Publishing L.L.C.
804 North Neil Street
Champaign, IL 61820

Phone: 1-877-424-2665
Fax: 217-363-2073
Web site: www.SportsPublishingLLC.com

To my daughters, Darian and Madison, whose bright, smiling faces make even the dullest day seem sunny.

CONTENTS

ACKNOWLEDGMENTS

M y mother, Francis Farrell, had always been on me about writing a book. I never thought the opportunity would come until I received a call in August of 2003 about doing a *Tales* book about the Pistons. Despite the chores of covering a professional basketball team on a daily basis and nailing down Rick Mahorn and Joe Dumars for interviews, the project finally got completed in June of 2004. My mom is a cancer survivor and one of my best friends. When I was home from college in the summer, we'd sit in the family room and watch *Little House on the Prairie* and lie to each other about not crying. I thank God that her cancer was detected early and that she's able to read this book. While working on the project, I never told her about it so it would be a surprise. I'd also like to thank Neville Britto, my junior high teacher, who got me interested in English and writing. He was a strong academic figure in my life, and I owe him a lot. Jim Leach, my high school journalism teacher, had doubts about my ability, but not any more. I'd also like to thank the doubters for driving me to higher heights and a successful career.

INTRODUCTION

In the 1980s Rick Mahorn and Joe Dumars represented the brunt and beauty of the Detroit Pistons.

Mahorn was the tough guy. He used his large rear end to knock potential scorers out of the lane, brutalize potential rebounders inside, and give the Pistons a presence that eventually led to the team's first NBA title in 1989. He had such an effect on opponents that they went into games thinking about fighting him instead of winning games. He was the Bad Boy, teaming with Bill Laimbeer to wreak havoc in the Eastern Conference in legendary battles with Boston and Chicago. In a game in Chicago a hard foul on Michael Jordan by Mahorn almost incited a riot, with Mahorn eventually tossing coach Doug Collins aside like a rag doll and drawing a suspension from Rod Thorn for his antics.

Conversely, Joe Dumars was considered the gentleman of the group. He came into the league as a relative unknown from McNeese State and was considered a defensive stopper, which got him into the lineup during his rookie season. By the time the team became an NBA championship contender, Dumars was one of the best shooting guards in the league as well as an All-NBA defender.

Together, in their own important way, they both were major contributors to the team's rise to glory.

Today, Dumars is president of basketball operations for the organization and has resurrected the team, putting together a unit that stunned the Lakers in five games in 2004 to win their third NBA title. While Mahorn continues to seek a head coaching job, he is a color analyst for the team and still one of its most popular figures, drawing crowds and conversation wherever he goes.

The two share their thoughts on the glory days, what happened during the team's decline and its resurgence back to elite status.

Chapter 1

OH ISIAH!

He spent his entire playing career in Detroit and had the greatest impact on the direction of a rudderless franchise as soon as he donned No. 11.

Isiah Thomas was the unquestioned leader of the Bad Boys during the Pistons' championship days. He was the great showman, the player who took the heat when things were bad and received much of the acclaim when the good times finally rolled around in the late 1980s.

"Zeke" or "Pocket Magic," as he was often called, led the Pistons to two championships and came close on two other occasions when the Pistons were stopped by bad luck more than the opposition.

Joe Dumars on His Backcourt Running Mate

"Zeke, Zeke, Zeke," said Dumars. "Whenever I talk about Zeke, there are so many issues and different things you can talk about with Zeke. If I'm just trying to sum Zeke up in a couple of sentences, it's almost impossible to do. I have to talk about basketball first, and if I talk about basketball first, I feel privileged that he and I got to play together in the backcourt for almost 10 years together. By far, he's the best player I ever played with. The best competitor I ever played with. I probably learned more from him, by just watching and observing, being on the court with him and being in the trenches with him, than any other player I played with.

"I say that there are OK players, then there are good players. Then there are players who are great, and then there are players who are special. I put him in that special category. There are not many people in that special category. I put Grant Hill in the great category, but he wasn't special. Isiah was special. Just from a pure basketball perspective, the best.

"He tells me all the time, 'Hey, Joe, when you find another backcourt that won to back-to-back championships and one guard was the MVP one year and the other guard was the MVP the next year, let me know, and then I'll tell you they are better than us.' He always says that, there's not another set of guards to do that. Until then, he says, we're the best ever."

Isiah Thomas (AP/WWP)

Getting Past the Celtics

Both Thomas and Dumars went through pain and joy together.

There was Thomas's bad pass that was stolen by Larry Bird and Boston in the 1987 Eastern Conference Finals. The Pistons lost that series in seven games after blowing that crucial Game 5 in Boston.

"Basketball-wise, that was the most devastating loss that I personally ever had and I know just about every other guy in that room ever had," said Dumars. "When you are fighting for something for a long time and you finally get to the point where you are to cross the threshold, and you trip and fall and you don't make it—that is more devastating than if somebody had taken it from you or beaten you to get it.

"I talked to Isiah about six o'clock the next morning. The way his house was constructed, he could walk out of his bedroom onto a balcony, and right next to the balcony was the slanted part of the roof of the house. He said he just crossed over and sat on the roof of his house at about four o'clock in the morning, just distraught.

"We had practice the next day. I will never, ever forget what happened. We really didn't do anything, we just came in and shot. We went to the Silverdome, and Chuck Daly said for everybody just to have a seat. That was unusual because usually when you start practice you don't go have a seat, you come to the middle of the court, say what you have to say and then you get started.

"Chuck talked about the disappointments of life and how you go through things, and this was one of those major disappointments and we had to keep it in perspective. The worst thing we could do was come back and lose Game 6. I thought he did a very good job of getting us to focus on winning Game 6. Win Game 6 and you're going to feel a whole lot better about yourselves. I just remember walking into the Silverdome that day and guys' eyes were still red like they had still been crying or were up all night and didn't sleep. Guys were walking around in a daze. 'How in the world could we possibly lose a game like that?' There was never any finger pointing. You never heard any guy, not one guy, say 'fricking Isiah' or 'what was going on?' If they said it, they said it privately. All we did was gear up and say you know what? We're the better team."

Making the Finals

A year later the Pistons finally broke through, reaching the Finals and taking a 3-2 lead on the Los Angeles Lakers in the best-of-seven series.

Severely twisting his ankle in the second half of Game 6, Thomas scored 25 points in the third quarter in one of the greatest individual efforts in Finals history. His 43 points weren't enough, and the Pistons lost the series in seven games with a damaged Thomas unable to contribute much in the final game, although Daly started him over Vinnie Johnson.

"That was probably the most heroic performance I had ever seen," said Dumars. "I wasn't there in 1971 or '72 when Willis Reed limped out there and did his thing. I was still in Louisiana, about seven or eight years old, so I didn't see that. I don't like to use those old cliches like gutsy and all that. I'm trying to think of a cool word or hip-hop word to apply to what he did that day. Maybe the word is phat. He was phat that day.

"I saw the guy's ankle. There was no question how bad that ankle was. That ankle was so swollen. He said, 'Joe D, look at here.' And I said 'Dude, man, I don't know how you're going to do it, but we got to go out there.' He limped out there. I'm talking about Game 7. That's why I say special about Zeke, and I mean that. When that cat was...When No. 11 put that jersey on in his prime and we'd walked out there... He was special out there on that court. I'll tell you what. There are a lot of great little guards out there now, and God bless them all. But if you put me in a foxhole and give me one of those little point guards— and all the ones out there like [Jason] Kidd and [Allen] Iverson and those boys are good—but give me Zeke in his prime. Man, Zeke was special."

A Career of Toughness

He was also tough.

There was the night in Salt Lake City when Karl Malone split Thomas's head open, requiring 44 stitches above his eye, leaving a scar he still has to this day.

"Zeke came back in that game and played, and all that was about was to let the other guy know, 'Not here, Chief,'" said Dumars. "Zeke was a tough little old guy. He'd take knocks, break his fingers and stuff and still tried to play. When you get into the special category, not only were you great on the court and tough and gutting it out with the ankle sprain, but Karl split my man's head wide open. Blood was gushing everywhere. The next thing you know Zeke was coming back out there. When he came back out there he wasn't the same. He was out of it, but just the fact he walked back out there. Guys talk about

Thomas played some of his best basketball in the NBA Finals. (AP/WWP)

being leaders, you have to show tremendous toughness. You can't be a leader just when things are going well for you. That's what that showed. The guy was team captain, leader, got his head split open, gets 44 stitches and walks back out there. That's your leader."

In 13 seasons he finished as the team's all-time leading point maker (18,822), field goals attempted (15,904), field goals made (7,194), free throws attempted (5,316), free throws made (4,036), assists (9,061) and steals (1,861). Heck, he's still in the top 10 in blocked shots (249) and rebounds (3,478).

A fighter, Thomas often took on big guys like 7'1" Bill Cartwright of the Chicago Bulls and Mahorn before he became a teammate. During a practice late in his career he broke a finger in a scuffle with teammate Bill Laimbeer when the big center elbowed him while he was nursing tender ribs. Don Chaney had to end practice and send the team home while Thomas went to the hospital.

Rick Mahorn on Being Traded to Play with Isiah

"I didn't want to be in Detroit. I was going to eat myself out of the league, and Jack McCloskey told me that. I was overweight and I didn't want to play. Earl Cureton and John Long called me Tubby. It really came to a head the year we lost to the Hawks in the playoffs in '86 and then in '87 we beat them with Adrian Dantley. I could hear them calling me fatass on the bench. I lost weight and got myself in shape and became the person I eventually became that year we beat Atlanta.

"Isiah jumped on my back after I left Detroit and was playing with Philly. When I was with Washington he assumed I hit him on a play when I threw a guy into him and knocked his teeth out before the All-Star game in '83. He thought it was me who hit him, but it wasn't. He did a tricky move. He went in air and slapped me in the face while he was in the air, and they called a foul on me.

"When I got traded to Detroit, Isiah called me on my private line in Connecticut and I knew his voice as soon as I picked up the phone. He said 'I'm so glad I don't have to run into your ass any more.' I didn't know I had gotten traded. I thought I was going to be a Bullet for life. I never wanted to leave there. So few players have that luxury of staying with one team. I wanted to start and end my career as a Bullet."

Into the Hall of Fame

In September of 2000 Thomas was inducted into the Hall of Fame in an emotional, tearful acceptance speech with his mother, Mary Thomas, and friends looking on.

"As a player, the Hall of Fame is like when you die you hope you go to heaven," said Thomas. "You never know if you're going to get there. You just keep living your life day by day. It's like making it to heaven. You're like 'Wow, God let me in.' The selection committee deemed my deeds worthy. I was very over-whelmed by the induction. There were really no words to describe how I felt. I was speechless and humbled."

Thomas said after his nomination: "I am a Piston for life. When you cut me open, I bleed Piston no matter where I am, who I'm coaching, what team I own. At the end of the day, I am a Piston. I am a Piston in terms of what the Pistons stood for."

Said Chuck Daly: "A glow kind of comes over you when you're inducted into the Hall of Fame. It's what defines your career."

A Deal Goes South

Still, one of the great questions that surrounds the organization is why was Thomas in Indiana coaching the Pacers and (briefly) working for former archrival Bird instead of sitting atop the Pistons organization with Joe Dumars as an administrator, coach or general manager?

That had been the plan ever since he reached superstardom in Detroit. He was the apple of owner Bill Davidson's eye. Thomas was like a surrogate son. He would be the one to run the organization after his playing days in Detroit were over. The two had reached that agreement, privately, with no word getting out about the deal until Thomas was through playing. That was the plan, anyway, but something went terribly wrong.

The culprit who leaked the story still may be operating at the Palace of Auburn Hills as Thomas toils in New York as president of basketball operations for the New York Knicks.

"I have great respect and admiration for Bill D.," said Thomas. "I always saw him as one of my mentors in terms of business. We were very close. That closeness made it possible for us to win."

While Thomas continues to try to rebuild his relationship with Davidson from a distance, the belief is that a high-ranking Palace official or family member let out the word of the deal between owner and player long before it was supposed to be announced.

Local newspapers and TV stations got wind of some deal between Thomas and Davidson and wanted to know what was going on.

What followed was an embarrassing press conference that announced nothing and left more speculation than confirmation.

The sordid mess left Davidson frustrated with Thomas, who to this day denies ever leaking the information to the media. After the press conference, all bets were called off involving his future with the organization after his playing days.

"I have no idea," said Chuck Daly about the events surrounding Thomas's fall. "I sat across the table from Isiah and I still don't understand what happened. He was like Mr. D's son. When Mr. D. went on vacation he didn't take me. He didn't take the general manager. He took Isiah. But don't worry about Isiah. He's got the charisma, intelligence and cunning to always land on his feet. Joe has the same characteristics; he's just more subtle about it."

Thomas realized that it would be Dumars instead of himself who would lead the organization into the late 1990s and beyond and told his running mate so.

Life After the Pistons

For a player who had rock star status in a hard-working, blue-collar town like Detroit, it was a blow to the Chicago native, who had taken Detroit by storm with his infectious smile, All-Star games, NBA titles and mental toughness.

After a stint in Toronto ended with Thomas resigning and leaving as the team's general manager, he landed in the broadcast booth and took over the Continental Basketball Association until he was hired as the Indiana Pacers' coach four years ago. To this day the CBA says Thomas left them high and dry after taking the job with the Pacers.

With a year left on his five-year deal, Larry Bird, who was hired to run the team's basketball operations in 2004, fired

Thomas for former Pistons coach Rick Carlisle, his former teammate in Boston and an assistant coach under Bird when he coached the Pacers. Bird had said the organization should never have hired Thomas in the first place after he resigned his post as head coach.

Thomas later declared that even if he had won the NBA title, Bird likely would have fired him.

Ironically, the Pistons hired Carlisle a year after he left Indiana. Before his firing, Carlisle posted consecutive 50-win seasons and led the team to the Eastern Conference Finals. In his first year with the Pacers, Carlisle led the team to 61 victories, a team record, and the Central Division title.

Two questions come to mind concerning Thomas. One is would the Pacers have been successful if Thomas was still coaching? The team won 61 games and posted the best record in the NBA under Carlisle. And two, will Thomas ever be a part of the Pistons organization again? That's a question that can't be answered right now.

Life After the Pacers

But in the meantime he has kept busy.

In December of 2003, he was hired to turn around the New York Knicks' fortunes. At the time they were 10-18 and slowly sinking out of the Eastern Conference playoff picture before the organization hired him as president of basketball operations.

He didn't waste much time.

By the time the dust had settled he traded seven of the 12 players on the roster and brought in the likes of Stephon

Marbury, a New York native, Penny Hardaway, Tim Thomas, Nazr Mohammed and Moochie Norris.

Eventually he fired head coach Don Chaney, for whom he had once played in Detroit, and hired Lenny Wilkens, the winningest coach in NBA history and also the one with the most losses.

Thomas accomplished his goal, getting the Knicks into the playoffs against the New Jersey Nets, where they were swept.

Isiah Thomas, Author

Thomas also found time to be an author, putting together a book titled *The Fundamentals: Eight Plays for Winning the Games of Business and Life*.

In it he wrote: "The lessons in this book came from Mary Thomas, my mother and role model, whose own life exemplifies determination and perseverance. I owe her everything. The best thing that has ever happened to me is my family: my wife, Lynn, and our children, Jose and Lauren. The most important figure in my life was my mother. I could sit for hours and listen to her stories and insights into human nature. She has uncanny power to bring out and focus on the best in people, even though she can intuitively detect the worst that is within them. She is the wisest, kindest, smartest, most loyal and fiercely determined person I've ever known.

"For a long time I planned on going into law and probably politics after basketball," said Thomas. "But it gradually dawned on me that I could have more direct impact and create more jobs for other people as a businessman. You'd only have to look at the long lists of businesses and investments that I've been involved in to see that I'm not one to pass up opportunities. I'm not impulsive about them. I consult with experienced business and investment professionals before committing my time, energy or money. Yet you could probably describe me as an 'opportunity junkie.' I look for those that will create even more entrepreneurial options so that one business breeds another, creating more jobs and widening the circle. I feel that if I'm not looking for new opportunities at all times, then I'm not doing enough. For me it's a way to keep my dreams alive.

I draw inspiration from the stories of the ranks of the Horatio Alger Society. I only wish that I'd known about these stories as a boy so that I could have shared them with friends and neighbors whose vision was limited by what they saw around them."

Rick Mahorn on Isiah

"Isiah was a great leader. He left it on the floor. He gave us a swagger and you always knew you had a chance with him on the floor with you.

"I've never been around anybody who wanted to win as much as Isiah. He took a beating, but he always came back. He was our leader, and when we took the floor we knew we already had a lot of teams beat."

Chapter 2

DAVE, BOB, AND NOT MUCH ELSE

In the years between 1967 and 1980, the Pistons had 11 losing seasons, but two All-Star performers that couldn't be blamed for the for the organization's bad times were superstar guard Dave Bing and Bob Lanier, one of the best shooting big men to grace the league. He was arguably one of the 50 greatest players in NBA history. The Pistons had their chances to improve, but they bungled a golden opportunity when they had three picks in the top half of the draft, including two in the top 10.

Were They the Right Three?

A floundering franchise in 1979, the Pistons had three of the top 15 picks in the NBA draft after posting a 30-52 record during the previous season.

Honoring Piston greats, including Bob Lanier (left back), Will Robinson (left front), Earl Lloyd (center), and Dave Bing (right). (Photo by Allen Einstein/NBAE/Getty Images)

With the unsuccessful Dick Vitale on the bench as the Pistons' head coach, they used the fourth pick in the draft to select Greg Kelser, who had starred with Magic Johnson at Michigan State, leading the Spartans to the NCAA national championship. With the 10th pick the Pistons took guard Roy Hamilton of UCLA, and with the 15th pick they stayed local again, selecting Michigan forward Phil Hubbard.

Key players who were drafted after the Pistons' threesome were:

• Center Bill Laimbeer to Cleveland with the 21st pick of the second round.

• Forward Earl Cureton to Cleveland with the 14th pick in the second round.

• Guard Jerry Sichting in the fourth round to Golden State.

• Guard Allen Leavell in the fifth round to Houston.

• Center and 7'4" big man Mark Eaton to Phoenix in the fifth round.

Armed with the three rookies, the Pistons sank to 16-66 that year, and Vitale was fired 12 game into the season.

Hamilton played just one season with the Pistons, started 10 games and averaged just 4.6 points per game. Obviously, picking him that high was a mistake.

Kelser played two full seasons for the Pistons and averaged 12.9 points per game before being traded to Seattle on November 21, 1981 for Vinnie Johnson. He had the best career of the three, playing in 305 NBA games and averaging 9.7 points per game and shooting 48.6 percent from the field. Kelser went on to become a color analyst for Fox Sports, doing Pistons and NCAA tournament games. His fluid delivery and knowledge of the game are tremendous assets for the networks, and he continues to have a bright future in that role nationally and with the Pistons.

Hubbard played 196 games for the Pistons and averaged 11.6 points per game despite a bad knee he suffered while playing at Michigan. He was traded along with Paul Mokeski on February 16, 1982, to Cleveland for Laimbeer and Kenny Carr.

So what the draft did was allow the Pistons to acquire two pieces to their championship puzzle. Laimbeer went on to become the team's starting center and inside force on a team that was hated for his rough play. Laimbeer was deemed the "Prince of Darkness" and was the most hated player in the league in the 1980s. But he was instrumental in the team's championship runs in 1988-89 and 1989-90 and now is a successful coach for the WNBA's Detroit Shock.

Johnson was nicknamed "Microwave" for his ability to come off the bench and score points in bunches.

He was the hero in Game 5 of the 1990 NBA Finals, hitting the game-winning shot with 0.07 left on the clock to give the defending champions their second straight title.

So maybe it wasn't a bad draft after all.

Dave Bing

Bing is still the best player to ever come out of Syracuse despite the emergence of NBA rookie Carmelo Anthony. During the late '60s, Bing was the running mate of Jim Boeheim, now the Syracuse head coach.

Bing was smooth. Bing was explosive. Bing had class. Bing was fluid and graceful. Bing just didn't have enough of a supporting cast to carry the Pistons out of what was then the Western Conference.

He played with the Pistons from 1966 to 1975. He was the second player picked in the NBA draft but was the league's Rookie of the Year after averaging 20 points per game.

In 1973-74 he led the Pistons to 52 victories, the most in the 26-year history of the team at that time. He was a seven-time All-Star and was the game's MVP in 1976.

He was able to rise over defenders and shoot his feathery jump shot while using his speed to whip past defenders on his way to the basket for easy scores.

He made first-team all-NBA in 1968 and '71. His No. 21 was retired by the Pistons after his playing days were over, and he was elected to the Naismith Hall of Fame in 1989 as the organization was at its zenith.

Dave Bing's Off-the-Court Greatness

Today Dave Bing is the president of Bing Steel and a regular attendee at Pistons games. Quietly, he sits about 10 rows up and close to the Pistons' bench. Very few have been better in a Pistons uniform. His business sense captured Dumars's attention early in his own career, and the two have become close.

"I know Dave better than I know Bob," said Dumars. "I think Bob is a very genuine, caring, sensitive, big man. He's a big man who seems to have a tremendously big heart. I honestly have, and this is no lip service, tremendous respect for guys like that, who have a sense of caring for other people. Bob has that. You see it in him every time you see him and talk with him and meet with him and hang out with him. He's not just saying things in front of the camera. Privately, he's saying the same things he's saying in front of the camera. When you meet people like that you just have to respect them. He's a major player in the NBA's Read to Achieve program, and that's all about giving. I think that those of us who have experienced whatever level of success we've experienced in life, you can't hold it for yourself and you can't take it with you. The only thing that's left to do is to pass it on to other people. I commend him for being that type of person.

"I have respect for Dave on several different fronts. I respect what he did as an athlete. He was an unquestioned legend and great NBA basketball player. He's so much more than just a former jock. He's a guy who had some vision and intelligence. He knows how to articulate well. He knows how to bring people together. He has so many different qualities that I respect and in some sense tried to emulate in just the way I carry myself. I don't really like to talk about role models a lot because I think

Dave Bing was one of the NBA's 50 greatest players, but his off-the-court career is even more impressive. (Photo by Ronald C. Modra/NBAE/Getty Images)

that term is overused, but he's truly what you would call a role model.

"It's not just about how good your jump shot was. There's a generation of people who know Dave Bing strictly as a leader, businessman, visionary and don't associate him that much as an NBA player."

Dave Bing, Role Model

Joe Dumars looks at Dave Bing as a model for the type of person he'd like to be.

"Ultimately that's where I want to get. People know that I played professional sports, but they see me as much more than a former jock. If that's all someone can say about you after it's all said and done, you haven't reached your full potential as a person.

"He started his company during his playing career. To me, he's one of the greatest African American athletes in the history of all professional sports in this country, not just basketball. You have guys who were visionaries, who were ahead of their time. Dave was a trendsetter. Mel Farr was a trendsetter. To establish your own business back in the late 1960s and early '70s when it wasn't as easy for African Americans to get started—my hat is off to those cats. They truly paved the way. That's why it's disappointing when you see these young athletes not taking advantage of what those guys set up. They fought when it wasn't trendy. If you fought the man back in the early '60s and '70s, you didn't know what the reaction was going to be.

"I really got to know Dave through business. We were at a General Motors business conference, and as per usual Dave and I talked for 20 minutes, and I would grant you we talked five minutes about basketball and the NBA. The other 15 minutes was strictly about business and what business we were doing. Of all the times I've spent with Dave, 90 percent of it has been about business and what we were doing. We have a common bond with basketball and we can talk about it casually, but by and large we talk about business, and that's what attracted me to him in the first place. I wanted to know. I was very curious. I wanted to know what road he took, how did he make that transition from great athlete, great NBA player, to successful businessman. I spent time with him and have had many a talk with him about that transition. My last five years in the NBA I started DTI, my business here. My talks with him during my career geared me to start thinking like that. His big thing was there's no possible way you can play 14 or 15 years in this league and the day your career ends and you wake up the next day and you say 'What am I going to do?' He said it's too late then. He said use your status when it's at its height to lay the groundwork, because people really want you then. When you're finished they still love you and like you, but you're not still playing. When you're still playing you can lay the groundwork for everything you want to do, and by the time you're ready to retire it's already laid. That's exactly what I did.

"The last five years I spent half the time playing and the other half studying business, briefcase in one hand and basketball in the other. I did it on the planes, at the hotels, on off days. I'd scheduled all my different meetings when I saw off days on my basketball schedule. It was all based around basketball. You just use basketball as a means to the end. It can't be the end. I got all of that from Dave Bing."

Adding Bob Lanier to the Mix

Lanier literally started his NBA career flat on his back.

The Pistons signed him to his first contract as he was in the hospital recovering from knee surgery suffered while playing in the NCAA tournament for St. Bonaventure in 1970.

Bob Lanier still represents the Pistons well. (Photo by Allen Einstein/NBAE/Getty Images)

At 6'11" and 260 pounds, he could shoot the left-handed jumper with the ease of a forward or guard and bull his way inside against smaller, inferior opponents.

In nine seasons with the Pistons, he averaged 22.7 points per game with a high of 25.7 points per game in just his second season.

In 959 NBA games he shot 51.4 percent from the field, finishing his career in Milwaukee.

The only time he averaged less than 20 points per game as a Piston was his rookie year, when he scored 15.6 per game.

When Lanier and Bing teamed to lead the team to 52 wins back in 1973-74, Lanier led the team in scoring at 22.5 points per game while Bing was second at 18.8. It was a high-scoring bunch of Pistons that included Curtis Rowe, Don Adams, George Trapp, Stu Lantz, Willie Norwood, and Chris Ford.

The Pistons averaged 104.4 points per game while allowing 100.3.

Their season ended in the first round of the playoffs when they lost to the Chicago Bulls in seven games with a disheartening 96-94 loss in Game 7 at Chicago Stadium.

The next year they were swept out of the playoffs in three games by Seattle, but in 1975-76 they advanced to the conference semifinals, losing in six games to Golden State after beating Milwaukee in three games in the first round.

Lanier now works for the NBA and resides most of the time in Arizona. He's instrumental in the league's Read to Achieve program, and not only is he an ambassador for the league but is still revered as a big man, with the soft voice, whom you didn't mess with on the court. Like Bing's number, Lanier's No. 16 has been retired and hangs above the Palace court and the team's practice facility.

Chapter 3

THE BAD BOYS

Assembling the Bad Boys

A longtime cellar dweller of the NBA, the Pistons started to put the pieces together in the early 1980s.

In 1981 they drafted Thomas and Kelly Tripucka, a high-scoring forward from Notre Dame, in the first round with the Nos. 2 and 12 picks.

In 1985 came a little-known guard from McNeese State who could score points by the bushel basket named Joe Dumars.

The next year a spindly seven-footer from Georgia Tech named John Salley was brought into the fold, and in the second round the team took a skinny 6'8" forward with big ears from little Southeastern Oklahoma State named Dennis Rodman.

The pieces were coming together.

On November 21, 1981 Greg Kelser was traded to Seattle for another guard named Vinnie Johnson, a scorer by nature who could burn you from the outside, but was strong enough to muscle his way past bigger players on the inside.

On February 16, 1982, the Pistons acquired Kenny Carr and Bill Laimbeer from Cleveland for Phil Hubbard, Paul Mokeski and 1982 first- and second-round draft picks. On June 17, 1985, Rick Mahorn and Mike Gibson were obtained from the Washington Bullets for Dan Roundfield.

In another key move on August 21, 1986, Tripucka and Kent Benson were shipped to Utah for Adrian Dantley, one of the best-scoring small forwards in the league and one of the best low-post threats for his size ever to play the game. James Edwards was obtained on February 24, 1988 when Phoenix sent just about everyone on the roster packing after a drug scandal left the franchise embarrassed.

The pieces were now in place, and assigned to guide this group was Chuck Daly, who was brought in during the 1983-84 season and eventually put together a staff that at one time or another featured Brendan Suhr, Brendan Malone, Dick Harter and Ron Rothstein.

Mahorn and Laimbeer added toughness and rebounding. Thomas, Dumars and Johnson could play either point guard or shooting guard and were interchangeable. There wasn't a better three-guard team in the league. Dumars worked his way into the lineup by playing great defense and quietly developing an over-all offensive game that made him dangerous in the low post or beyond the three-point line.

Thomas controlled the offense as the point guard. Dantley was a half-court nightmare for defenders to the point that he was nicknamed Teacher. Salley and Rodman became the X-factors. They could come off the bench and change the tempo of the game with defense for transition dunks. If Thomas or Dumars were off, Johnson would come in and put on a dazzling display of spinning, darting moves that would leave defenders shaking in his wake.

The Bad Boy Persona

The Pistons officially assumed the nickname on January 18, 1988. Thomas was upset about a fine and suspension handed down to Mahorn, and he made a declaration.

"If they want to make us out to be a Raiders-type of basketball team, then we can become a very, very aggressive type of team and let people know that this is the game we play."

The story went that not long after Thomas's statements, Al Davis, the owner of the Raiders, sent the Pistons a package of paraphernalia, which they wore before coming up with the Bad Boys T-shirts of their own.

After Mahorn was fined by Rod Thorn, the league's dean of discipline, Mahorn said: "As far as I'm concerned Rod Thorn can kiss my ass."

Thorn now runs the New Jersey Nets operation and has a better-than-average relationship with Dumars.

GM Jack McCloskey said at the time that promoting such an image was a mistake, but that nothing would change as long as the team was doing well, which meant first place. McCloskey and the organization were fined $29,000 during the 1988-89 season, more than three times more than the Portland Trail Blazers, who were fined $9,500 that year to rank second.

Rick Mahorn on His Suspension

"I got suspended 1986-87; the year All-Star game was in Chicago. It was a game that we were playing Denver and I had to sit out. I got suspended because I knocked Michael (Jordan) on his ass and pushed Doug Collins out of my way at Chicago

Stadium. They were giving out desk tablets that night and they were throwing them at me when I was leaving the court. Those things hurt. They were slinging those things all over the place. Rod (Thorn) and I are cool. Rod understood a lot of the things back then. We played a physical style of ball. He had to do what he had to do. We went to New York after that and Laimbeer and I put this sign on the wall of his office with crazy glue and took a picture in front of it. The sign said "This office is donated by the Detroit Pistons Fine Club." Everybody was scared to tell him who did it, but he laughed and said it was one of the funniest things he had ever seen. It wasn't that Rod didn't like us. He loved our style. It embraced him. I guess that's how he used to play. Rod would levy the fine and that would be it. I thought the Pistons did a good job of keeping it in the right perspective and not letting it get out of hand. They caught me flipping somebody the finger during the national anthem and Rod called me and said, 'Were you flipping somebody the bird during the national anthem?' I said no. He was cool."

Returning to the Playoffs

In Daly's first year the Pistons made it to the playoffs for the first time since 1976-77. But the Pistons lost in an electric, high-scoring, high-energy five-game series to New York when Bernard King literally carried the Knicks' offense on his back in Game 5 at Joe Louis Arena, beating the Pistons 127-123 in overtime.

Refusing to go away quietly, Thomas had scored 16 points in a span of 94 seconds in regulation that eventually sent the game into overtime. His performance left both sides grabbing for superlatives.

"With all sincerity it's too bad someone had to lose that game," said Hubie Brown, coach of the Knicks at the time and the current coach of the Memphis Grizzlies. "Isiah Thomas's effort in the fourth quarter was a staggering punch to us. I've been around a long, long time, and I've never been in a game like that."

It was part of the team's maturing process.

The next year the Pistons advanced to the second round, where they took Larry Bird and the Boston Celtics to six games before losing.

It was just the start of the most heated playoff series throughout the 1980s between the Pistons and Celtics.

The organization suffered a setback to their championship hopes in 1985-86 when they lost in the first round to Atlanta, with a 114-113 double overtime loss in Game 4 sealing the Pistons' fate.

About this time the team's rough-and-tough image was starting to put other teams back on their heels with Laimbeer boarding and brooding on the court while Mahorn used his toughness to intimidate defenders.

Taking the Next Step

The Pistons made their first trip to the Eastern Conference Finals in 1986-87 where they lost to the Celtics in seven games. The series included the fateful pass by Thomas that was stolen by Bird and Johnson and Dantley bumping heads in the third quarter of Game 7. Johnson and Dantley bumped heads while

Mark Aguirre, sitting between Bad Boys Rick Mahorn (left) and Dennis Rodman (right), was considered a valuable addition by Chuck Daly. (Photo by Jonathan Daniel/NBAE/Getty Images)

diving for a loose ball. Some Boston trickery helped keep both on the bench long enough to help the Celtics.

"We didn't have team doctors traveling with us at the time, and the Boston doctors kept saying Vinnie had a concussion and couldn't come back in the game," said Mahorn. "You have to give it to Boston. They were smart. Vinnie kept getting up saying he was OK, and their doctors kept saying he was hurt. That's when we started bringing Ben Paolucci and doctors started traveling with us on trips. At that time we used to rely on the other teams' doctors. AD had a concussion. Anybody hitting Vinne's head would have a concussion. They knew how to pull that leprechaun out whether it was in the doctor's office or them hitting you in the back of the head with a basketball."

Dantley spent the night in the hospital with a concussion. Johnson returned after applying an ice pack to his neck, but he missed the final 7:21 of the game with an injured neck and the Pistons were doomed.

The Dantley/Aguirre Trade

During the 1988-89 season, the Pistons traded Dantley to Dallas for Mark Aguirre. Management saw Dantley as a player who had reached his peak and whose best years were behind him.

His moves were being anticipated by opposing teams. Dantley was considered selfish and greedy and infatuated with money, according to an article written in the *Detroit Free Press*. Daly had tolerated Dantley, but clearly a change was needed. Aguirre, not exactly a choirboy for peace and harmony, was considered an upgrade from Dantley.

After the trade, Dantley's mother, Virginia, unloaded against Thomas, whom she blamed for the trade since Thomas and Aguirre were friends and Chicago natives.

"You shouldn't blame Jack McCloskey; he's not the one," she said. "It's that little con artist you've got up there. When his royal highness wants something, he gets it."

Ironically, when Thomas was elected to the basketball Hall of Fame, Dantley's high school coach, Morgan Wooten, also was elected the same year. Dantley was at the ceremony in Springfield, Massachusetts, but Thomas and Dantley supposedly never came in contact with each other. To this day Dantley always believed that he should have won a ring with the Pistons' first championship team.

Using the Bad Boy Image as a Weapon

By now the Bad Boy image was in full bloom, and it wasn't uncommon to see Laimbeer or Mahorn or Rodman getting under an opponent's skin and just often nearly inciting a riot. After Dantley was let go, Aguirre wasn't exactly welcomed with loving arms, but the Pistons were on their way to 69 wins and their first NBA title.

"When we would fly into cities the day before we'd play a team, I would grab the newspaper, or I would grab the newspaper the next morning the day of the game," said Dumars.

"Invariably, you would always read about their biggest and strongest guy talking about 'I'm ready for the Bad Boys, and I won't back down and I'll fight any of those guys...' You knew right when you were reading it we had these boys beat already. This guy is talking about fighting. Doesn't he know we have a game tonight? The coach is saying, 'My guys won't back down and we're going to get just as physical as them,' and they would talk about everything but winning the actual basketball game. They wanted to show that we weren't going to test their manhood. You knew they couldn't just be concentrating on basketball and winning the game. For myself, I never felt any pressure to act a certain way. If you asked any of those guys on that team about toughness, I think they all would put me right up in that group. I just didn't feel the need to be out front with the altercation and the hype and all the stuff that was going along with it. I just wanted to be the quiet, tough guy on the team. I think every team needs different personalities to win. I don't think you can have 12 of the same personalities. I don't think you can have 12 loud, rowdy, outspoken, on-the-edge guys. And I don't think you can have 12 reserved, nobody-says-a-word guys. I think I was just part of the mix. I felt like I was just as tough as anyone else on the team. You have to understand during those times I was averaging almost 20 points a game. Zeke and I were the leading scorers on that team. I had to worry about guarding young Reggie Miller, young Clyde Drexler, young Michael Jordan, and a young Mitch Richmond. You're talking about guys who were dropping 25 every night.

"When we won the championships in '89 and 1990, we had gotten Mark Aguirre for Adrian Dantley. You have to remember Mark was averaging 25 points per game or more his whole career. But when he came to us he didn't care about that. He just wanted to win. Mark's still one of my favorite people in the game. He wouldn't trade anything for those titles. What he did to his game to help us win showed me a lot about the kind of players I want.

"I didn't have time to get physical and get into these altercations. I was playing against skilled, great players. I had to be physically tough. I had to be mentally tough. I didn't have time for all that other stuff. If I was just a big bruiser and was scrapping to get six points and eight rebounds, then yeah, maybe I could have, but I was expected to drop 25 on the other end as well.

"Rick Mahorn and Bill Laimbeer took the brunt of it. What that did was free the rest of us up to play. Once or twice a game a big old boy would thump somebody pretty bad and a couple of technical fouls would fly and the other team's bench would lose their mind. You'd see everybody over there ready to fight. The next thing you know Zeke and I were going to the line the next eight times down the court because the other team was trying to be physical. There were a lot of nights I went up to the referee and said, 'Hey, listen, I don't want to get hurt out there because these guys are trying to be physical with Bill and those guys. Just understand that's where I'm coming from, I'm just trying to play.' As soon as they'd hit me, the referee would call a foul and I'd say thank you.

"Laimbeer and Mahorn were tremendous for the Bad Boy reputation because they took the brunt of all the heat. While the rest of the team worried about how to get back at them, Zeke and I were giving them a steady diet of 20 and 25 points on them, just feeding it to them. The next thing you know there's a minute left and we're up 14 and they're wondering what happened.

"When I was younger I resented how people perceived us. Man, we were a great team. It wasn't about being thugs. If that was about being thugs, you could go out and get a bunch of thugs and win a world championship. We were putting up numbers. The first year we won it, we averaged 106 points per game. As time went on I realized a lot of the people that resented it or wouldn't give us credit didn't have a clue as to what it took to get it. You're talking about some writer across the country who might have seen us play once or twice in person, and he's making a judgment on who we are as a team. As you get older you realize most of the people who are judging you don't have the slightest idea of what it takes to be a world champion. So why am I getting upset because this guy over here isn't giving us credit? Whatever, dude. Have another beer."

Practice Makes Perfect

Mahorn said some of the best basketball the team played was in practice.

"Man, we'd go at it," he said. "Chuck would always tell us that you earned your minutes in practice. The games would be

Rick Mahorn played tough whether he was hurt or not. (Photo by Rick Stewart/NBAE/Getty Images)

easy because you didn't have to go up against the guys you were competing against for minutes. Sometimes the coaches would leave and we'd come back to the gym and take care of unfinished business. We'd hit each other, bang each other, but we were able to keep it to a point where we didn't hate each other."

Their First Final

The following year, 1987-88, the Pistons finally broke through, beating the Celtics in six games to advance to the NBA Finals for the first time in franchise history. Taking a 3-2 lead into the Forum for Game 6, Thomas exploded for 25 points in the third quarter, but along the way severely sprained his ankle. Despite 43 points from Thomas, the Pistons lost Game 6, 103-102, and with Thomas a shell of himself in Game 7, the Lakers still only prevailed by three, 108-105, with a phantom call on Laimbeer against Kareem Abdul-Jabbar sealing the visitors' fate late in the game.

"Zeke got hurt, but I was hurt too," said Mahorn. "I had a ruptured disc. I shouldn't have even been playing. If you look at it, Zeke was our captain. Your focus is going to go on the captain, and we could've won that too [Game 6]. You figure he gave us a great third quarter and we needed to carry it through in Game 7. Sometimes as a coach you second-guess what you want to do. I think Chuck did it right by not only starting me, where I could have sat and got surgery and sat on the sideline and they could've gotten another player. Chuck wanted to keep me there. It was the same thought in Game 7. Isiah had carried us this far, you just can't go ahead and sit him. He had gotten 25 points in that quarter playing on a bad wheel, and we had a healthy

Vinnie on the bench. Vinnie was ready to go. We had to commend Chuck for sticking with his player. That's why people loved to play for Chuck Daly. He never doubted his players. I think after he went to Orlando and figured out how this new generation was, he just didn't want to deal with it. There was a lot of selfishness, but there was a lot of unselfishness on our part as players. We sacrificed our games for everybody to win as a team."

Running the Gamut

"We had to beat Cleveland, Indiana and Milwaukee, too. Cleveland had a great team—Larry Nance, Mark Price, Brad Daugherty, Craig Ehlo." said Mahorn. "They worried me. One year they were right on our heels and we were playing them at the Richfield Coliseum. Price was having a great game and I told Isiah to bring him to me off a pick. I hit him and he fell to the floor. I think he suffered a concussion. They weren't the same after that and we ended up winning the division.

"I think it was like the Western Conference is right now in the East. On any given night you could lose between Boston and Cleveland and Indiana or Atlanta. Philly was good. The Knicks. We had a lot of foes. We didn't even beat the Knicks the year we won the title. They beat us four-zip in the regular season. Chicago knocked them out. They had the mental game on us. I don't know what it was about New York. It wasn't that they had the center in Pat Ewing...They just beat us. I guess it was the mystique of New York. We just couldn't beat them. They beat us twice at home, once convincingly. We could probably have been mentally equipped to beat them if we had seen them in the playoffs, but it was easier to play Chicago because we knew we could punk them."

The Dirty Label

"When people said we were dirty it didn't bother me. I didn't care. People came to the games a lot because of us, because we brought the essence of basketball into the game. The same thing the older players did, we brought it back. It was physical. It wasn't on the verge of dirty or cheap, because if it were on the verge of dirty or cheap there would've been a lot of people hurt—broken legs and broken arms. We played the game to the edge in order to stay focused. We were so focused in on what we wanted to do...Our practices were better than games. We got so tired of playing against each other. Playing against new meat was easy. Our competitive and mental edge came from practice. Our practices weren't that long. Our practices were an hour at the most. Chuck didn't want practice to go any longer. One thing about Chuck is he told us at the beginning: play for your minutes. I wasn't starting at first. I was coming off the bench. I was the power forward/center. I'd come in for Laimbeer. I was the first big man. The first five games (in 1987) they started Salley for five games and he didn't score, so they started Sid Green. I was the backup center and the backup power forward because I knew both positions. Some guys didn't learn two positions. I'd go in the game and Sid Green and Laimbeer would be in there with me, and I'd move to center when Sid Green came back, or whoever Chuck would put in at the power forward. Eventually they asked me to start. I said OK, but I was kind of mad because during practice I wanted to play

*John Salley was another one of the versatile members of the Bad Boys'
potent frontcourt. (AP/WWP)*

against the first team and whip ass. Walker D. [Russell] tells me
to this day that Chuck should have never taken me off the second team. It was Vinnie and me. And we'd be bumping and
shining those boys. Vinnie was the best guard and I was the best
big man. Walker D. was the off guard and we'd beat the crap out
of the first team. I ended up playing really good that year in '87.

The following year I got hurt. The first time I got hurt was on the West Coast trip.

"We had a combination of guys who could play three positions. You could see a lineup out there of James Edwards, Laimbeer and myself. It's kind of like the Pistons this year because I could put Rasheed [Wallace], Memo [Mehmet Okur] and Ben out there at certain times. All of a sudden you have a long front line. Laimbeer would do the dirty work. We really didn't have an inside threat other than AD (Dantley). We just beat you with dribble penetration and when you tried to double-team our guards, they'd kick it out. Salley was a shot blocker. Worm was a defensive guy who got rebounds. We were one of the best offensive rebounding teams at that time. It was fun. Our big men, we did our jobs. We did what we had to do. We played tough defense. We would run a go-play. If Laimbeer wasn't in there it would be a 1-5. If I wasn't in there it would be a 1-4. I knew I had to roll to the basket and Lam would just stop and pop.

"Our margin of victory the first championship year was about seven points per game. I knew we shut people down when it counted, but I never realized we gave up as many points a game as we did. We scored a lot of points. Nobody could stop our pick and roll. If you look at Karl Malone and John Stockton, they did it for 18 years. Nobody can stop the pick and roll. It's the best old play in basketball. We had guys with basketball savvy who knew how to go off the pick. We knew our roles and what we had to do. The whole team had basketball IQ. If a guy rolled, we knew where to go and where to stop. We knew our guards were going to shoot, so we knew at what times to go to the basket. If anybody does it well they can really get a lot of things out of it.

Vinnie Johnson (center) provided a spark off the bench. (AP/WWP)

"We knew how to slip a double-team if the guy was going to jump out quick to make the defense honest. We knew how to do it if a guy was going to switch. We did it where the guard could get in the middle of the paint. We did so many versions of the pick and roll in one play."

Bonding with Teammates

"I didn't like Laimbeer at first, but we'd go in the steam room or the sauna after practice and have a Bud. Or we'd sit with Vinnie and have a couple. Joe would be in there and we'd end up just laughing at everything. The whole thing was we enjoyed winning. Winning killed all ills. We were always pushing for the other guy. That was the fun in it. A lot of times you find some haters in the game. We liked each other and we encouraged each other to do well."

Comparing the New Championship Generation with the Old

"On the current team Ben would have been about the only one who played. Rasheed might have gotten off the bench. I'm not knocking his ability, but he wouldn't have shot a three-pointer. To me he would've been like William Bedford—big guy who wanted to shoot threes. No, you had to get in the paint because you wouldn't play. We had guards to do that, but it's a different game now. I think Ben would've got off the bench with his ability and desire, but with his offense it would've been hard for him to get off that bench. Our big guys knew how to post up. Worm could score. There was a reason why Worm could average 28 points in college and act like he couldn't shoot a jumper. Worm could score. He knew it wasn't his role. I could score, but it wasn't my role. My role was to come in there, set the tone, set picks, and play defense.

"We sacrificed for winning the championship. The whole focus was not to make the playoffs. C'mon; that was too easy a goal. You want to win championships as a player. You don't want to be on the team just to make the playoffs every year. I wanted to be on a team fighting for a championship every year. If I didn't make it this year then I'd come back next year with the same goal of winning the championship. That's when you become greedy as a player because you want to win championships. You can make all the money in the world...When I was in Philly, I gave Allen Iverson my championship ring when we were starting the playoffs during the lockout. He just sat there and his eyes just lit up. I told him it was better than all the jewelry he had on. You can lose all of your jewelry but you would always be a champion. That ring was a symbolic gesture. I think he became very hungry and thirsty after that. They made the Eastern Conference Finals and lost to Indiana that year, then the next year they made it to the Finals. I think he appreciated that because he had a lot of guys on the team who genuinely loved the game, and Larry Brown coached that team. We had Aaron McKie and Theo [Ratliff] and Tyrone Hill and Matt Geiger and Larry Hughes, Nazr Mohammed. We had guys who would sacrifice their game because we had guys who could score. They didn't learn that until after I left.

"When you have a good group of guys, chemistry becomes the key. You don't want to mess up the chemistry because it's so fragile. It may be one player you take away that collapses the group and the chemistry you have. As a GM or a coach you don't know who that guy is. When you lose him that's when you know that was the guy that kept everything together."

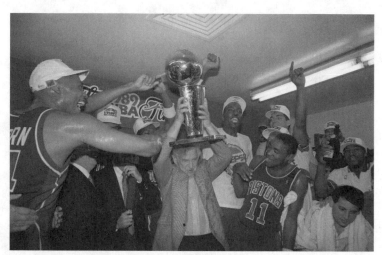

The Pistons bounced back from a wrenching loss in the 1988 Finals to sweep the Lakers the following year. (AP/WWP)

Reaching the NBA Peak

By '89 the Pistons were ready to capture their first NBA title, and Dumars was the catalyst. They swept the depleted Lakers in four games with No. 4 winning MVP honors.

He scored 22 points in Game 1 at the Palace, then added 33 in Game 2 with 26 in the first half. In Game 3 at the Forum he was relatively quiet in the first half, but exploded for 21 points in the third quarter and finished with 31 as the Pistons took a commanding 3-0 lead with a 114-110 victory.

Quiet in victory or defeat, Dumars was now starting to get noticed as one of the game's solid all-around guards.

"It's like people were just finding out, 'Oh, hey, he can play.'"

Despite all the attention, he still didn't have much to say.

"Joe was always the background guy," said Daly. "He never demanded much attention. He was so easy to coach. It was unfair he didn't get the attention. He was so quiet, really a star's star, because he was a thinking man's player. He thought the game through and was a winner. He was getting into business and figuring out how to be successful in the community while he was still a player. He has carried that over into turning the Pistons around."

He put the finishing touches on his MVP performance by scoring 23 points in the finale, a 105-97 victory as the Lakers' starting backcourt of Magic Johnson and Byron Scott could only watch from the bench because of injuries.

"When I look back it seemed the mental and physical pressure was so great," said Thomas. "It's a long process. It wears on you because you get knocked off so many times and the hardest part is picking yourself back up and starting the climb all over again."

There were times, like the pass against Boston that was stolen by Bird, that Thomas wanted to give up, but the fight in him, the fight that he learned from his mother Mary, kept him going.

Chapter 4

RIVALS

Boston Trickery

According to Mahorn, the Celtics had ways of getting to the Pistons.

"We should have won three or four championships. We had some tough series with the Celtics. We'd be in a hotel in Boston and they'd turn the hot water off in our hotel rooms. People would call our rooms at three or four o'clock in the morning. In the summer the Boston Garden would be burning up in our locker room and they'd turn the heat on. We didn't have any hot water to shower with after games.

"We played there one year and there was a broken window and cold air was coming into the locker room. They said somebody threw a rock into the locker room and broke the window. If that was the case there should have been glass on the floor by the window. There was no glass inside. All the glass was outside the window, meaning somebody had broken the window from the inside. Between that and cold water... Cold water in the win-

Laimbeer (40) and Mahorn (44) were constantly battling with Boston's frontcourt. (Andrew D. Bernstein/NBAE/Getty Images)

ter, hot water in the summer. I think Mike Abdenour used to return the favor by turning up the heat in their locker room when they came to our place."

Trash Talking

Larry Bird was a well-rounded player. According to Mahorn, he could score, rebound, pass, and talk trash with the best of them.

"I think Larry Bird talked more trash than anybody else, just because he was country and from French Lick...He knew how to talk some trash. It was kind of nice because it made it more competitive. I'd guard him and he'd say 'May-Horn is on me, May-Horn is on me. He'd say my name wrong on purpose. I'd say, 'My name is Mahorn. Don't be messing up my name.' Then he'd come back again and say, 'May-Horn is on me.' It was fun. I think the competitive juices really came out when it was Boston. We wanted to beat them bad. Them dudes...They beat us in every facet of the game, then when they couldn't beat us in the game, they'd beat us mentally. They just had our number. You have to figure how to get past that. We got past it as a collective unit because it got to a point where we knew we were better and we had to prove to ourselves that we were better than them."

When the Pistons and Celtics' rivalry was at its peak, they could draw crowds of more than 60,000 fans in the Silverdome. (AP/WWP)

Rick Remembers Isiah's Pass

"The bad pass with Isiah happened in Game 5 that year. We could've lost that series after Game 5, but we kept our focus. Isiah threw the pass away, and that was out of character because I was the designated guy to take the ball out of bounds. I was a better big-man ball handler. If I got caught in the backcourt and there was a jump ball, I'd have a good chance of winning it because teams weren't going to bring their big men to guard me bringing the ball up the court. On that play I was looking at Chuck waiting to get my orders. Chuck was calling a timeout. The thing was he [Thomas] was trying to get the ball in real quick. We could've gone back home and lost Game 6, because if we dwelled on what happened last night and what happened in Game 5, we wouldn't be prepared for Game 6. As a unit we

Bird and Isiah were key players in the playoff history between the two teams. (AP/WWP)

knew we had to win Game 6 to force a seventh game. We thought that we should've won Game 7 as well, but Boston came in there and played their A game and we lost one of our horses that was carrying us [Vinnie Johnson]. We could have said could've, would've, should've, but we got what we deserved.

"We won the mental game in Game 5. We knew we could beat them, because we had them. We gave it away. It would've been different if they had beaten us, but we had them and we gave it away. That's when we won the mental game. We knew we could beat them. In Game 7 we could have beaten them. If we had played them another series after that we would've beaten them. All they did when they stole that pass was prove they were fortunate to win. We came back collectively as a team and blasted them here in Detroit because they knew they weren't going to win here, and we forced a Game 7."

The Bulls Rivalry

After the Celtics were dispatched, it was time for the now-established Pistons to fight off a team of upstarts. Mahorn remembers dealing with the Bulls.

"The thing about Chicago was Chicago had Scottie Pippen and Horace Grant and Bill Cartwright and B.J. Armstrong. We had their number. For one thing, Pippen got the headache. AD [Dantley] gave him the headache the first year. Then Mark Aguirre destroyed him the next year. Mark, being from Chicago, he was a thug, plain and simple. You weren't going to bust Mark Aguirre because he was going to stand up for his. I used to laugh at how they used to talk about Horace Grant. Then they were saying Michael was just going to shoot the ball all the time, and he did. That was his job. Once Michael became that consummate team player...It was real scary."

Joe Dumars on Facing Michael Jordan

"I always tell people don't mistake brashness, boasting and hype with being tough," said Dumars. "Most of the time the guy who brags the most and talks the most and brags the loudest, the first thing people say is that's a tough guy. I truly believe, walk softly and carry a big stick. I believe in that.

"Whenever we got ready to play Michael Jordan and the Bulls and he was in his prime... Here's a guy who had 50- and 60-point games enough where you knew it could happen on any given day. He could easily walk out there and drop 55 on you. I knew a lot of guys in the league who didn't want to see Jordan. I took the opposite approach. I couldn't wait. I looked forward to playing him because I knew I was going to play as hard as I could, because he forced you to. Whatever the best I had in me, I'm going to see it from myself today. He forced you to dig as deep as you can.

"I looked forward to it. I never, ever, ever dreaded playing against him, because I always felt like I could compete with this guy, every night. Yes, he had some 25- and 30-point nights, but I was of the mindset I was just not going to lie down and let him get 35 or 40. The funny thing about it, there were nights that we got real physical with each other. Games got physical and tension was high and maybe frustration set in. A couple of elbows here and there, but nothing out of control. A short shot here, hit you with a shoulder in the chest. In 14 years of playing against him, I think maybe once there was an exchange, not an altercation. Once, he went up for a shot and I bumped his legs in midair. I'm quite sure he said, 'Joe D, you could hurt me like that.' And I said, 'Yeah, you're right, my bad.' In 14 years that was it. We never said a word, even when I would have big games against him, scoring and defending, I would never, ever utter a sound. I think that was as beneficial to me against him as anything. These other guys were yakking and talking and his pride kicks him and he goes crazy. I never said a word, ever, not a confrontational word. There were times, and I would do this intentionally, too, we'd walk out on the court and it was, 'How are Debbie and the kids doing?' 'Good, Mike, how are Juanita and the kids doing?' Great; great. All right, let's do it; OK, let's go. Boom! And we may not say another word the rest of the game. Or he'd make one of those spectacular moves, and maybe during the next free throw and he and I were at halfcourt and I'd say, 'That was a pretty nice move. It was OK.' He'd say, 'All right, thanks, man.'

"He was great. We never had one confrontational word. Defense is a mentality. Competing against somebody like that, it's a mentality. You either have a chance to win before the game is ever played or the game is already lost before the game is ever played. If you've lost before the game is played, then he's going to drop 60 on you. I'll tell you what also helped. Because I had such a good relationship with the referees, I was allowed to be more physical with him than anybody else. I would watch him play two days later and guys would barely touch him and the whistle was blowing. I know two nights earlier I had been hammering him. I heard him say this to Jess Kersey one night: 'Hey, Jess, Joe's a great guy, but he fouls too.' I remember telling Jess, 'Jess, how about this? Michael Jordan is complaining about foul calls? I said man. Armageddon.' We all laughed. Jess laughed, Michael laughed and I laughed. The fact that I was able to play him physical and get on him and bump him and bang him and not have fouls called on me... For the average guy that was a foul. The only thing I would do is I would go and say to the referee real quietly; I'd slide up beside him and say, 'You know, I think he's good enough that he doesn't really need any help with those type of calls. He has a pretty good future in this league. I think he's going to make it in this league. You don't have to help him with that type of call. That's a Michael Jordan call right there. Be fair. That's all I need. If you are fair I have a fighting chance.' They'd say OK. That was it. I'd just walk away.

"Hey, I'm in the game now. You only respect people who you know are going to stand their ground. You're not going to respect somebody that's going to fold like a cheap suit the minute things get tight. You only respect people you know aren't going to back down. That's why I never said anything."

Rick on MJ

Mahorn said the key in the early days for the Pistons was to gang up on Jordan.

"One man wasn't going to stop Michael Jordan," he said. "You can't stop Kobe or Shaq. You better have a whole lot of help defensively. One man can't stop one man in the NBA. You have to have a total team effort. A lot of guys say they can, but please. If you have one of the best centers to ever play the game, you have to have an awful lot of help.

"We all played our men man-to-man, but we had a pattern where we knew how to play defense. We knew everybody's weaknesses, so if they beat us we switched and we knew what we were going to do. If I switched out on Michael I knew I was

Michael Jordan and Joe Dumars staged some epic battles on offense and defense. (AP/WWP)

going to make Michael go to his right hand. He would've killed us if I didn't. I knew I had help on that side. Michael, the competitor he is or was when he played, learned to hit that mid-range jumper. That's where he learned to pull up and hit that mid-range shot. You could see a lot of similarities in Rip Hamilton's game. A lot of people don't work at that craft much anymore.

"It's the same with Kobe. Kobe perfected it. Michael started it. Michael learned from the older guys what was going to make him a better scorer. You don't have to go in there and take a beating. Do the mid-range jumper. He's already up in the air before people were thinking about coming after him. As long as Joe kept him dribbling with that left hand for three or four dribbles we were OK. Once a guy can do three dribbles, then he was basically ours. Anything past three dribbles you knew some trouble was going to happen because we had time to come with our help defense, but if you did one dribble and went up in the air... There's no recovery for the defense."

Chapter 5

DENNIS RODMAN

Joe Dumars on Dennis Rodman

"Dennis was a freak of nature from a physical standpoint. He was a special kind of athlete. He was 6'8", slim, strong as two horses, wiry but strong. I don't know another guy who could guard every position on the court. I saw him guard Hakeem Olajuwon and block a shot at the end of the game to preserve the game for us. Michael Cooper was close, but you couldn't necessarily put him on centers back then. Dennis could guard everybody on the floor. I was thinking one time during a stretch Dennis guarded Michael Jordan, a guard, James Worthy, a forward, and Olajuwon, a center. That's a freak of nature, that guy's type of ability. He could ride the stationary bike for a half-hour after the game was over and he had played 40 minutes. He could grab all the rebounds. I'd love playing with him because he'd get those offensive rebounds and run and hand it back to you. I said hey, keep that guy out there. He wasn't even looking at the rim. Offensive players would love playing with him. He'd run get the rebound, take a couple of dribbles and hand it to you and then run back under the basket. That was my guy. He truly was an X-factor because he could affect the game in so many ways. On a particular night he could get every offensive rebound. He could affect a game defensively by taking three, four, or five charges. He could affect a game by diving into the stands and getting the crowd energized. He could affect a game by running the fast break with those left-handed dunks he used to do. At the end of the night he might have six points and completely affected the whole game. That's special. That's why Ben Wallace is special. The guy could have six points, and everybody would leave shaking their heads talking about him.

"They're similar in that way. There are not that many guys in the NBA who can do that. You have Ben right now. Jason Kidd can be like that, then after that you have to really start stretching. You don't see guys like that often. Jason Kidd is a MVP candidate, Ben Wallace is a back-to-back Defensive Player of the Year. Those guys are huge. You don't often find that kind of guy."

Rodman's Versatility

Rick Mahorn marveled at Rodman's ability to guard three positions.

"He could face certain centers," said Mahorn. "He could guard small forwards and power forwards. A lot of people don't know this, but Dennis could score. You don't average 28 points per game in college without being able to score. Dennis did his job. He rebounded, blocked shots, grabbed rebounds and did the dirty work. Dennis and Mark Aguirre would really go at it

Dennis Rodman (AP/WWP)

in practice. Dennis would get a busted lip and minutes later he'd be right back out there."

The Later Days of Dennis

Once Chuck Daly stepped down as Pistons coach, Rodman's psyche took a turn from fragile to freakish.

His behavior became more disturbing to the organization. Once he arrived to work out at the Palace in the wee hours of the morning with a shotgun. Management thought a psychiatrist might help.

Disinterested and hard to reach emotionally, eventually Rodman was traded to San Antonio for David Wood and Sean Elliott. There, the different-colored hairdos and even stranger behavior started. However, Rodman's rebounding continued to be his one constant in the 128 games he spent in San Antonio. In 1993-94 he averaged 17.3 boards his first year in San Antonio and 16.8 in his second year before he was traded to Chicago for Will Perdue on October 2, 1995.

Rodman wore No. 91 in Chicago because the two numbers added up to 10. Squeezed between Michael Jordan and Scottie Pippen, the out-of-control Rodman helped the Bulls to three of their six NBA titles, but the alcohol, photographer kicking and referee bumping was too much even for the title-driven Jordan and coach Phil Jackson.

When the Bulls decided to disband the team, Jordan retired for a while, Jackson left and eventually landed in Los Angeles, and Rodman drifted to Dallas before he was released.

Dennis Rodman was a Bulls nemesis until he joined the team for the second three championships. (AP/WWP)

Dennis After Basketball

Since his last NBA game, Dennis has been in a series of brushes with the law, a marriage that had him living in one house and his wife another, and some failed comebacks to get back into the league. Even as late as January he talked of coming back and hooking up with an NBA team.

He also has managed to stay in the limelight, appearing for one season on ABC's *Celebrity Mole.*

Chapter 6

LIFE AFTER THE BAD BOYS—

Rebuilding with Jerry, Grant, and Lindsey

For the Pistons, trying to reach the Finals again after the consecutive championships proved to be a difficult task. A number of talented players came through Detroit, but none could deliver the franchise to the promised land, although one was part of the third championship team's rotation.

Stack Attack

From the moment Jerry Stackhouse was traded to the Pistons along with Eric Montross for Aaron McKie and Theo Ratliff on December 18, 1997, things got lively around the Palace.

The 29-year-old Stackhouse didn't mind speaking his mind, to teammates, to coaches, his entourage on the sidelines, or anyone else who would listen.

He demands your attention because of his high-powered nature on and off the court. Before he left Detroit for the Washington Wizards, he not only had set the team's single-season scoring record with 2,380 points and a 29.8 average in 2000-2001, but he had gone through coaches Doug Collins, Alvin Gentry, George Irvine and Rick Carlisle.

On April 3, 2001, Stackhouse became the Pistons' all-time single-game leading scorer when he poured in 57 points at Chicago's United Center in a 110-83 Detroit victory. It was one of the strangest nights in team history, because by the end of the game, Bulls fans and players were cheering Stackhouse's every basket. In the house that Michael Jordan built, Stackhouse left the arena with the single-game scoring record for an opponent or Bull, surpassing even Jordan. When a local beat writer slammed the evening's events in the *Sporting News*, Stackhouse took the article and threw it in the reporter's face.

"Jerry was volatile with his emotions," said Dumars. "Jerry wasn't a bad guy; he was an emotional guy and he would react inappropriately at times, but Jerry has a good heart—a great heart. I can deal with guys who have had problems or have had bad things happen, but I can't deal with a bad guy. There's a difference between a guy who has issues, and has had bad things happen, they've done bad things, but they're not bad people. Jerry Stackhouse, in terms of his heart, he was a good guy. Jerry played behind me for three years. I used to practice against him every day; I know him. He and I used to ride to the airport together. We'd go out to dinner on the road. We'd talk about life and family, how much you love your parents and what you want to do for them. Bad guys don't sit around and talk about that kind of stuff.

"Jerry wore his emotions on his sleeve, whereas Grant Hill didn't. A lot of times the public, in general, is drawn to people who wear their emotions on their sleeve. Sometimes it works the other way. I think that's what happened with me. People have good vibes with me and I never wore my emotions on my sleeve.

"A tennis example would be Pete Sampras as opposed to John McEnroe. To me Pete Sampras is the greatest tennis player ever. In the general public of tennis fans, they identify more with John McEnroe. He was one of the top three or four players of all time, but people usually gravitate towards him more. He wore his emotions on his sleeve, the outburst, throwing his racket. The fans, they like that outburst. Sampras never really did any of that. He was No. 1 in the world for six years. That won't ever happen again.

"When you talk about Grant and Jerry, I put it in that context."

Battling with Teammates

Before he left Detroit, Stackhouse also had put a couple of teammates flat on their backs.

First there was Christian Laettner, a Duke grad and four-time Final Four participant. Stackhouse put aside the fact that he was from North Carolina and Laettner went to hated Duke when the team signed him in 1998. However, when the 6'11" Laettner kept teasing Stack about losing money in a card game during an airplane ride in 1998-99, Laettner felt Stackhouse's wrath in full force. Irked to the limit, Stackhouse leaped from his seat and pummeled the taller Laettner, nearly landing him atop the Pistons' play-by-play announcer, George Blaha.

The incident left the organization embarrassed and Laettner with a black eye. The organization's public relations department tried to deny the incident happened, but when Laettner emerged from Gentry's office with a black eye, the jig was up.

Neither commented on the scuffle as word got out, but Stackhouse was the undisputed winner on appearance alone.

Stackhouse made it 2-0 a year later with Jerome Williams as his second victim.

The Pistons had barely made the playoffs with a 42-40 record after firing Gentry with 24 games left in the season.

When Grant Hill injured his foot, the Pistons quickly fell behind 2-0 against Miami with the deciding Game 3 in Detroit on April 29, 2000. On the Friday before the game, Williams lamented to the media about how the team couldn't change their style of play despite Hill being out.

"It's too late for that," Williams announced.

When Stackhouse was asked about Williams's comments, Stackhouse replied, "Jerome who?"

He repeated it a couple of more times before disappearing into the locker room.

The story goes that Williams approached Stackhouse while the two were getting dressed to leave the team's practice facility. Supposedly taking a threatening pose, Williams looked down on Stackhouse before the shooting guard slammed him into a cubicle and started joustling with Williams.

The team lost the next day, and the following year Williams, a popular figure in Detroit with his Junkyard Dog routine, was traded to Toronto along with Eric Montross for

Jerry Stackhouse (AP/WWP)

Corliss Williamson, Kornel David, and Tyrone Corbin on February 22, 2001.

Connecting with the Community

To Stackhouse's credit, he gained more local popularity than even Grant Hill while a Piston. Detroit fans could relate to Stackhouse. He didn't mind being out and about and held a yearly celebrity wheelchair basketball game with the proceeds going to diabetes research. He had lost a couple of family members to the disease.

He opened his house to the media and teammates before the start of his last season in Detroit, welcoming Carlisle and Co. to a pre-training camp barbecue. His gorgeous Michigan home, which could be seen from Orchard Lake, was highlighted in *Cribs,* a cable show that took the average American inside the homes of the rich and famous. Stackhouse continues to be both and is still one of the most colorful players to ever wear a Pistons uniform.

The last two seasons he toiled for a losing team in Washington. Stackhouse had knee surgery in the off season and barely played this past year. When he said late in the year that he was shutting it down because of the pain in his knee, management told him no and told him to keep playing. However, when the Pistons played Washington a game before the season finale at Toronto, Stackhouse was nowhere to be found on the Wizards' bench or in the locker room.

He didn't make the trip.

Over the summer the Wizards traded him to Dallas for Antawn Jamison, another former Tar Heel.

Sir Grant

Other than drafting Isiah Thomas in 1981, there was no greater anticipation than in 1994 when the team used the No. 3 overall pick to select Grant Hill.

Hill had won two championships at Duke. He was 6'8", athletic, the son of former pro football player Calvin Hill and high-powered attorney Janet Hill. He was well spoken, good-natured, good-looking, and the plan was to surround him with enough talent to bring the team back to the glory days of the mid-1980s and early 1990s when the team celebrated two championships.

Can't Carry the Team

Despite the fact that Hill made the All-Star team every year, the Pistons couldn't reach that next level. Many Pistons fans pointed to Hill as the culprit even though the numbers don't add to the argument. The only time Hill didn't average 20 points per game was his rookie year when he came in at 19.9 points per game.

"When he came into the league...If I was the commissioner of the NBA, I look at Grant Hill and I say he represents everything I want my league to be about," said Dumars. "He was a tremendous athlete. He was very bright, educated, good citizen, good spokesman. Everything that you would look for in an athlete, Grant was. In his time here in Detroit he represented all that was good about the NBA. On top of that, Grant's a good guy. He's misunderstood in a lot of ways and has obviously caught the worst break of his life with the ankle injury. We have

talked since he left, and I told him 'of course we would've wanted you to stay,' because I knew we were going to turn this thing
around. I want him to play, I want him to be healthy, I want
him to be happy. I want his family to be happy. You wish that
for good people. He's a good guy. He made a decision that was-
n't popular with a lot of people here, but he's a good guy."

In his final season as a Piston, 1999-2000, Hill hired a
shooting coach and averaged a career-best 25.8 points per game,
shot 48.9 percent from the field and shot 79.5 percent at the
free throw line. However, in the four appearances in the playoffs
the Pistons made during his stay, they never won a series.

Grant's Reputation

Locals accused him of being "soft" or unable to make the
big shot in key games. Unlike Thomas and Stackhouse, Detroit
fans had difficulty, at times, relating and feeling a sense of
warmth towards Hill.

"This is what I liked about Grant: he was a superstar NBA
talent," said Dumars. "He had the physical tools and the game
of an MVP of the NBA. He had the humility and the mentality, a lot of times, of a rookie free agent trying to make the team.
He never really, to me, carried the persona of 'I'm a superstar,
treat me as such.' Grant always wanted to be one of the guys.
I've seen a lot of guys who were caught up in being stars. 'I want
this and I want that.' He never was like that. That's why I will
always have good feelings about Grant, because he was never
about that ego or attitude. You can't dislike a guy like that. You
might not agree with everything, but you can't say he's a bad
guy."

He said all the right things and represented his family and the organization with class, but he was a shirt-and-tie upper middle class star in a blue-collar town. For his career in Detroit, Hill averaged 21.6 points per game and shot 47.6 percent from the field. It's no secret that head coach Doug Collins made life so miserable for Hill that he contemplated retiring from basketball before the organization saved him by firing Collins during the final half of the 1997-98 season. Collins literally begged Hill to help him save his job, but to no avail. When the Pistons were swept out of the playoffs by Orlando during the 1995-96 season, Collins said nary a word to Hill over the summer, instead opting to cozy up to Allan Houston, who had a great playoff series against the Magic, even outshining Hill.

In his final season as a Piston, Hill suffered a foot injury. He missed the final playoff game against Miami as the Pistons were being swept aside by the Heat. Needing surgery, Hill was part of a sign-and-trade with the Orlando Magic while still on crutches. Wanting out of Detroit, he was traded for Ben Wallace and Chucky Atkins, virtual unknowns at the time. While Wallace has gained notoriety as one of the NBA's great rebounding power forwards and twice has been named Defensive Player of the Year, Hill's career has taken a free-fall.

The Aftermath of the Trade

Three years later there's no disputing which team got the best of the trade because of Hill's injuries.

Hill hopes to make a return to the Orlando lineup this season after yet another surgery, but he'll have to do it without Tracy McGrady, who was traded to Houston along with Juwan

Howard, Reece Gaines and Tyronn Lue for Steve Francis, Cuttino Mobley and Kelvin Cato. While he was never given the full credit he deserved for the work he put in as a Piston, there was never an indiscretion or controversy surrounding Hill's stint at the Palace.

If he never plays another game, he has already been successful. He has a beautiful wife in Tamia and a baby girl, but to get back on the floor and end his career in a manner befitting his talents is something Hill deserves.

"I played with Grant for five years; he was my neighbor," added Dumars. "But he made his decision before I took over. He told me he was sorry, but I realized he was committed. I understood. But I remember telling Grant, 'Boy, we're going to be good one day.'"

Dumars was right.

I'm Not Isiah

Lindsey Hunter grew up idolizing Isiah Thomas. At Jackson State he wore No. 11 in honor of Thomas. So when the Pistons drafted him with the 10th pick in 1993, there was every expectation that Hunter would come in and run the team the way Thomas did in his heyday. With Allan Houston with the 11th pick, the Pistons, even Thomas, thought the team had their backcourt of the future with the 6'6" Houston and the 6'2" Hunter.

"When Lindsey first came here his game was nothing like Isiah's," admitted Dumars. "Lindsey is a spot-up point guard. He's cut out of the mold, more athletic, of a Steve Kerr, a John Paxson, a B.J. Armstrong. He's a point guard who is kind of off

Grant Hill got the Pistons back into the playoffs, but the team could never get out of the first round. (AP/WWP)

the ball. He's not your prototypical guy who you can put the ball in his hands for 40 minutes and say run the show and make sure everybody is involved. That never was Lindsey. You didn't know that until time had passed.

"As that time was passing he was taking knocks every year for not being the next Isiah until people realized that's not who he is. I think Lindsey's best year was when he and I and Grant Hill started on the perimeter and Grant and I handled the ball most of the time. He spotted up and shot. He didn't handle the ball that much that year. Either Grant had it or I had it. It was unfortunate that he got that comparison when they were totally opposite players.

"I think it affected his confidence. I'm sure he heard and read it. He took shots. No matter what people say, athletes' confidence is fragile. There are not a lot of guys who can wake up and read something negative about themselves and fight through it and be successful in spite of that. You get so caught up into what somebody has said that it hurts you and the way you perform. He was here in the same town, same position and he played one year with Isiah. It wasn't like it was two or three years later after Isiah had left. They were right there. That's an awkward position for a guy to be in. He idolized Zeke, and that was going to be a tough situation for him to succeed. I think he has a better shot now, after 10 years in the league, of having some success here this season than at that particular time. The expectations aren't there. We're not going to thrust him out there."

A Different Set of Skills

Hunter had set the Jackson State scoring record as a senior with 48 points against Kansas and averaged 26.7 points in his last season, taking more than 700 field goal attempts for the SWAC member.

The problem was Hunter wasn't the decision maker with the basketball that Thomas was. He was better with the ball in someone else's hands on the fast break so he could be open on the wing for jump shots.

Hunter was as quick as lightning and could get to the basket and dunk on a taller opponent if the situation called for it. However, he wasn't nearly the passer Thomas was and his role was often changed with the revolving cast of coaches who sat on the Pistons' bench after the departure of Chuck Daly after the 1992 season.

In his rookie season Hunter averaged 10.3 points per game and shot 37.5 percent from the field. The next year he played just 42 games because a broken bone in his right foot. In seven seasons with the Pistons, Hunter, playing alongside Dumars as a shooter and ball handler, averaged 11.2 points per game, handed out 1,635 assists and shot nearly 40 percent (39.8). He turned out to be an excellent on-the-ball defender and solid three-point shooter, but the shoes Thomas left were too big for him and most of the point guards who wore a Pistons uniform to fill.

Hunter's best scoring season was 1996-97, when he averaged 14.2 points per game and shot 40.4 percent from the field.

Hunter often looked at the way Philadelphia used Allan Iverson and thought his game was better suited to that style with Iverson being fed the ball in the open court to maneuver around the defense instead of setting others up.

Traveling Around the League

On August 22, 2000, Hunter was traded to Milwaukee for Billy Owens. A year later Hunter was traded to Los Angeles, and he picked up his first NBA championship ring, starting off and on for the injured Derek Fisher while mostly coming off the bench to help the L.A. defense.

After a year in Toronto, Hunter was reacquired by the Pistons for Michael Curry. It was a short move for Hunter, who had kept his home in suburban Detroit during the years he played with Milwaukee, Los Angeles, and Toronto.

The championship run with Los Angeles was a bittersweet year for Hunter. The summer before heading to L.A., his brother Tommy, a freshman-to-be at Jackson State, was killed in a one-car accident near Murrah, Mississippi.

Hunter, who owned a funeral home with his uncle, handled his brother's arrangements.

Although he turned out not to be the player who led the Pistons to two championships, Hunter carved out a successful career in the league despite the fact that he was a scoring guard in a point guard's body. His quick hands, quick feet and quick jump shot proved beneficial.

Hunter was involved in a trade that sent him to Boston on February 19, 2004, but six days later he was back in the red, white, and blue when the Celtics waived him, as planned, and he was re-signed as a free agent by the Pistons.

Lindsey Hunter (AP/WWP)

Picking up Another Ring

After the move that sent Bobby Sura and Zeljko Rebraca to Atlanta and Chucky Atkins to Boston and brought Rasheed Wallace and Mike James to Detroit, Hunter now found room off the bench to help the team, especially defensively.

James and Hunter were called the team's "pit bulls," sent into the game to attack the opponent's opposing guards and wreak havoc with steals and turnovers.

"That's our job," said Hunter. "I know I can score in this league; I've proved that. I just want to be able to come off the bench and pressure the ball and come up with steals so we can convert the turnovers into easy baskets. It was so much fun winning a championship here."

Despite the fact that he had a strained medial collateral ligament and tendonitis, Hunter was the defensive catalyst off the bench for the Pistons, often coming up with a big steal or key stop to inspire his teammates.

Hunter was the only Piston with a championship ring, but many of his teammates refused to look at it when he brought it around during the playoffs.

They wanted to win one on their own—with his help.

As the Pistons went on to defeat the Lakers in five games and win the championship, no player smiled more or enjoyed the moment more than Hunter.

"To come back here and win the championship after being drafted by the Pistons is a greater sense of accomplishment for me than when I won it with the Lakers," admitted Hunter. "I knew once we got Rasheed we had a chance to win it all. I think we all had just one single purpose in mind: that was to come together and win this thing. We didn't care who was the leading scorer or who won the MVP. We just wanted to win the championship. It's a feeling I'll never forget."

Hunter mulled retirement before the title run, then decided he had more basketball left in him, signing a two-year contract with the Pistons during the off season. However his career ends, he reached one milestone with Thomas: both have two championship rings.

Chapter 7

THE COACHING
CAROUSEL

Daddy Rich

Chuck Daly, known as Daddy Rich when he roamed the Pistons' sidelines, is still the most successful coach in Pistons history. He won 467 games and led the team to two NBA titles. He was hired on May 17, 1983 while working on the Philadelphia 76ers' broadcast team. Despite the fact that he hasn't coached the Pistons since the 1991-92 season, he said fans still associate him with the Pistons, something in which he takes great pride.

Daly was a player's coach. Minutes were earned in practice, not in games. If you wanted to beat out Vinnie Johnson or Bill Laimbeer or Mark Aguirre, you would have to do it in practice, because the team was so deep and talented that everyone wanted to play and deserved to play.

"Chuck was great at motivating players," said Dumars. "He knew the right things to say and he had a great coaching staff with him."

In assessing one of his favorite coaches, Mahorn said: "Chuck's philosophy was come in and do your job. You practiced like you played. He said, 'Look, we can be here for an hour or three. I don't have anything to do.' He figured if you had a veteran ball club, they wouldn't want to be at practice any longer than one hour, but in that same hour we might play a pickup game, and that team might lose, and we'd wait until Chuck left and play another game. We weren't finished. There was some bad blood. We wanted to finish the game. Sometimes Chuck would call practice because our practices were so competitive. They were games. We had game situations. I think that's what made us even better. We ran game situations. There weren't any friends. There were friends after. If you got hurt, you just kept on going. We turned it off when practice was over, but it depended on the person. People would carry a grudge. I didn't carry a grudge, because I was inflicting more pain than anybody, so I didn't care. If you didn't like it, I didn't care. We learned to like each other. A lot of times we'd go in the sauna or after practice we'd go over to the Silverdome or at the Palace and sit in the steam room and sauna."

Learning from Daly

Rick Mahorn was briefly a head coach, and he owes any success to Daly.

"From my coaching standpoint, everything I took, I took from Chuck. In my head-coaching stint in the CBA, I took everything from him. I took all of his philosophy that I gathered and information I gathered while I played for him. I think Chuck made the statement that I would make a great head

Chuck "Daddy Rich" Daly led the Pistons to their first two NBA championships. (AP/WWP)

coach, and I was still playing. Chuck and I never talked. We never had a conversation. The only time we talked was at the beginning of the season. He told me my role and what he expected of me. Once he told me what I had to do and I started, I said cool. The only time Chuck talked to me was if there was a situation that wasn't beneficial. Mentally, I was ready. I started to set the tone of the game, and if I came out, he said be ready to go back. You could never be disappointed as a player if a coach tells you what he wants. Half the guys now, I think, in the league, they expect more instead of giving more. You don't expect anything. You give more to get back and get the opportunity.

"In my coaching stint in Atlanta as an assistant, I tried to instill what Chuck taught me, but when you have someone who thinks he knows everything...I don't know it all. I'm always going to be a student of this game. That's just life. You learn something new every day. That was a great experience for me, but the best was the CBA. I really wanted that ring. I wanted that ring more than the ring I already have. I wanted a CBA championship ring and I was determined to get it. To take a team from last place to first place was commendable for my guys. It wasn't me. We had the same guys who were in last place. We didn't add any new players. I just had those guys believing we could beat anybody.

"The head coach takes all the pressure. You take all the heat, but it's good if you can deal with that pressure. Chuck could. I enjoyed being a head coach in the CBA. I would never call a player out personally. I would confront them privately as a human being. That builds more respect. If a player gave me what my team needed, I gave him what he needed. The NBA needed players who knew how to play basketball. I love it when you have guys thinking they could beat the world, and Chuck was that kind of coach."

Winning Without the Accolades

Despite his fantastic success in Detroit, Daly never won a Coach of the Year award. When he coached the Pistons, he was the oldest coach in the league. He had spent seven years in high school coaching, eight as a college head coach and four as an NBA assistant coach. He worked as a furniture loader, construction worker, and bouncer in a bar in Tokyo. He was always a snappy dresser, pacing the sidelines in well-tailored suits and a full head of hair. He never searched for the spotlight. He gave the players the credit and tried to keep an ornery bunch of players led by a feisty point guard in check. He and Thomas had their problems. The relationship didn't always go well, and there would be times when the two wouldn't speak except when Thomas was on the floor.

Once Daly walked up to Thomas and asked him what his best attribute was. Thomas replied: "I'm a leader." So Daly told him to go lead.

Since Daly's departure, the Pistons have gone through seven coaches, with Larry Brown currently at the helm.

Replacing Daddy Rich

After Daly left, Ron Rothstein's no-nonsense, tough defensive approach lasted one season. The team finished 40-42, and Rothstein, now an assistant with Rick Carlisle in Indiana, was gone.

Next was Don Chaney.

"Don was a nice guy," said Dumars. "It would have been hard for him to win with that team because we were in transition. We had some older players and some younger players trying to blend in. It was a tough situation."

Chaney lasted 164 games, winning just 29.7 percent of them. The team's futility did lead to the drafting of Grant Hill, who would eventually help get the team back into the playoffs.

Chaney was let go for Doug Collins, one of the brightest minds in the pro game. He immediately lifted to the Pistons to a 46-36 record and the playoffs. He was driven, and he pushed everyone around him, including the players and coaches. Practices were intense, and Collins was a tireless worker.

A Brief Return to the Playoffs

The playoffs were short and bitter for the Pistons. Shaquille O'Neal and the Orlando Magic swept the Pistons in three games. Allan Houston emerged as a star in the series, and Collins gravitated to him that summer more than he did Hill, something the former Duke star noticed when he reflected on his relationship with Collins.

The next season, 1996-97, the Pistons won 54 games under Collins, but lost to the Atlanta Hawks in the first round of the playoffs in five games.

Forty-five games into the 1997-98 season Collins was unceremoniously let go and Alvin Gentry, one of his assistants, took his place.

"Doug was a brilliant bench coach," said Dumars. "Nobody knew Xs and Os any better than Doug, but the organization decided we needed to go in a different direction."

Gentry proved to be good with the media and tried to carve out his own niche as the team's head coach. After finishing 16-21, he led the team to the playoffs in the strike-shortened season, going 29-21.

However, the Pistons went down in five games to the Hawks, again failing to get out of the first round.

Gentry lasted 58 games into the next season before the Pistons decided to make a change. Assistant coach George Irvine reluctantly took the job after saying initially that he didn't want it.

Irvine won 14 of the team's last 24 games, and the team sneaked into the playoffs. However, Hill went down with a foot injury, something that still plagues him to this day. Detroit eventually was swept out of the playoffs by the Miami Heat.

Rick Carlisle

When Dumars hired Rick Carlisle he seemed to have hit the jackpot. Carlisle was young, innovative, charming when he wanted to be, and hungry to prove himself.

The first year he turned the Pistons around, winning 50 games and earning Coach of the Year honors, and helped Corliss Williamson claim sixth man honors while Ben Wallace was picked as the league's Defensive Player of the Year.

"The identity of this team right now is that of a very balanced outfit built around a lot of very good and talented players," Carlisle said at the time. "Rather than having one or two real stars of note, we have eight or nine really good players. I don't think there's anything wrong with that. I liked the idea of not having to rely on one player. We can wear people down. We can spread it around. Other teams can't just focus on one guy."

Rick Carlisle led the Pistons to consecutive 50-win seasons.
(AP/WWP)

Dumars liked the fact that Carlisle was a young, energetic coach.

"He's a former player, he gets out there and gets dirty," Dumars said at the time. "He doesn't coach from a tower. He gets right down there in the mix. I knew all those things would be good attributes for him to be a good coach."

The Pistons advanced to the second round of the 2001-2002 playoffs, where Boston eliminated them in five games.

The Rookie-Veteran Divide

Over the summer and during the playoffs, Dumars intently watched the development of New Jersey rookies Jason Collins and Richard Jefferson and how Nets coach Byron Scott used them during the regular season.

Dumars drafted a talented young forward in June from the University of Kentucky named Tayshaun Prince, and Mehmet Okur came from Europe for his first season in the league. He also traded Jerry Stackhouse over the summer for a younger, better mid-range shooting guard in Richard Hamilton. Dumars had hoped Carlisle would use the two young players the same way Scott had used Jefferson and Collins.

It didn't happen.

Relying too much on veterans Cliff Robinson and Michael Curry, Carlisle painted himself into a corner by not letting his young players make mistakes during the regular season while learning to play the NBA game.

Dumars never once demanded Carlisle play the two rookies, but he was quietly frustrated that neither was developing at the rate he wanted.

In late January owner Bill Davidson met with Dumars and Carlisle and supposedly railed on his coach as being stubborn for not playing the youngsters.

Carlisle had to make a decision: do what his boss wanted or play the veterans who gave him a sense of security on the floor.

He played his veterans.

He also criticized members of the organization about everything from scheduling to statistics to not being overly friendly with season-ticket holders. However, the team kept winning, posting another 50-win season and claiming the Central Division title for the second year in a row.

However, a long playoff run was in jeopardy when the Orlando Magic built a 3-1 lead in the first-round best-of-seven series with Game 5 set for the Palace. When Curry got into foul trouble in the third quarter, Carlisle was forced to play Prince, and the rookie responded at both ends, scoring while shadowing high-scoring Tracy McGrady. Sparked by the young forward, the Pistons rallied to become just the seventh team in league history to rally from a 3-1 deficit and won the series in seven games.

Both Prince and Okur played well in the next round against Philadelphia, only adding fuel to the fire that Carlisle should've played both more during the regular season. By the time the Pistons had been swept by New Jersey in the Eastern Conference finals, Davidson had already decided that he wouldn't renew Carlisle's contract after the following season, which would have made him a lame duck coach the following year.

Looking at Larry

Just after the Nets beat the Pistons, Brown had resigned his head coaching position in Philly, and Davidson was interested in hiring the longtime coach to take over his young and growing team.

In a shocker, Dumars was sent to hire Brown and fire Carlisle, which he did on May 31, 2003. Three days later he hired Brown.

"On the court he did a good job with us," said Chauncey Billups of Carlisle. "But off the court he just didn't treat people the right way. It caught up with him."

Of Larry Brown, Dumars said: "You want to have somebody who's fanatical about details, about doing it the right way. For example, we went through a play offensively, moved the ball around, moved it around, threw it inside, scored and he stopped the play and just got after guys. You would've thought we had thrown it out of bounds on a turnover. Even though we scored, it wasn't how we were supposed to run a play. I've never seen a coach in all my years who would stop a play like that and just rip into guys about not executing the right way. All too often we'll say, 'Oh well, we scored anyway.'

"His point was, 'Yeah, we scored in practice the other day, but when we get into a big game and we call this play and we have to execute it... If I've allowed guys to freelance and get away with it they'll do it a crucial time, and it's going to cost us.'

"That's who he is. If you want a story to epitomize him, that's it."

Brown's Resume

Brown also came to the Pistons well traveled, having worked for ABA Carolina and Denver before and after it entered the NBA, along with New Jersey, San Antonio, the L.A. Clippers, Indiana Pacers, and Philadelphia 76ers.

Brown was inducted into the Hall of Fame in 2002.

He led Kansas to the NCAA national championship in 1988 and became the first coach to win NCAA and NBA titles when the Pistons beat the Lakers. As a player, he spent five seasons in the ABA and was on the 1969 ABA champion Oakland team. He also coached the 2004 U.S. Olympic Team.

His greatest NBA season before coming to the Pistons was in 2000-2001, when he led the 76ers to the NBA Finals, where they lost to the Lakers. He was named NBA Coach of the Year that season.

The Detroit job was much different for Brown, who was used to taking over bad teams and turning them into contenders.

"I never came into a situation where a team had a winning record and generally had its core players in place," said Brown. "From that standpoint I felt like a stranger. I didn't want to infringe on what Rick tried to do. I had a lot of respect for what he has done here, and I felt like it was a learning process for me."

Family Affair

One of Brown's assistants was his brother, Herb, who coached the Pistons in the early 1970s. Herb is 67, and mom Ann Brown, who is 100 years old, couldn't be happier. Younger

The well traveled Larry Brown finally won an NBA title in Detroit.
(AP/WWP)

brother Larry has been in the spotlight for years, arriving on the radar screen as a point guard from the University of North Carolina and rising through the ranks as a player-coach in the NBA.

"When I arrived at North Carolina I was a high-scoring guard from Long, Beach [New York]," said Brown. "All I remember is at practice, when I shot the ball the gym was quiet. When I passed the ball, the coaches applauded and encouraged me. That stuck with me."

As a player, Brown was considered both unselfish and great. Milton Brown died when Herb was 10. He died in a local hospital of a brain aneurysm. The boys woke up the next morning and, as was Jewish custom, all the mirrors in the house were covered. Their uncle told Herb of the news, but six-year-old Larry was kept in the dark. He was sent away during the funeral.

"My dad was away all the time; he was a traveling salesman, so it wasn't all that unusual for him to be gone," recalled Larry. "For a while they didn't tell me, but I knew. I hear about it now, how he impacted my life. You never replace your dad, no matter what. But I had my older brother. I had my mom's family. They all treated me like I was their child. They all made unbelievable sacrifices for me. We lived on top of the bakery. I remember sleeping with my grandfather half the night and having to learn how to sleep between snores. I never thought I was missing out on anything. I mean, how many shoes can you wear? Or shirts? I just wanted to play ball."

And coach it.

Getting the Team into Place

When Brown arrived in Detroit, he took the time to get to know every player's strength and weakness. Every player on the roster got a chance to show what he could do to the point where Brown had a hard time whittling his rotation.

He tried to get the team to run early in the season, but when the result was bad decisions on the fast break and confusion in the open court, Brown started calling plays until the guards felt more comfortable with his system.

"I am more comfortable as a coach, because I know more of what guys are capable of," Brown said as the season went on. "I was asking them to play the way I coach and the way I was taught, but sometimes that's not in your best interest. I've always felt that the strength of a coach is to recognize what guys are capable of doing and put them in situations where the chances of them failing are not too great."

Brown talked of playing the right way so much that it became ingrained in the players' minds. Chauncey Billups was the point man and received the most criticism when he played the wrong way and ended up winning the NBA Finals MVP because he played Brown's right way.

Chapter **8**

Rebuilding Take Two

For Pistons fans, it was nice keeping Joe Dumars in the organization. But the good will would only have lasted so long—Joe needed to build a winner.

The Plan

"You have to have a vision and you have to have good planning," said Dumars.

"This is something Bill Davidson and I talked about before I took over. He came to me and said, 'Hey, I'd like for you to do this. I think that you're the person to get us back.' I asked him what was he looking for out of me. He said he was looking for my vision. 'I know you have a business background. I know you understand people. I just think that you're perfect for this role.'"

"You have to have a vision about where you want to be even before you get there. You can't get there and say this is where I wanted to be. You have to know beforehand. You have vision, planning, discipline and good people around you. You have to make the right decisions about the right people. You can do all that, and if things don't fall into place for you, it doesn't matter. We've had excellent vision, great planning, excellent discipline, and we've made some good financial moves. We've caught some breaks, and fortunately enough, when you catch a break, you have to be in a position to take advantage of it. That's why I think both things have to go hand in hand."

Making the Transition from the Court to the Front Office

For many players, moving from competitor to management can be trying. Dumars used his last experience as a Pistons player to shape his franchise blueprint.

"The last team that I played on in '99 was mainly a team of complementary players. I realized that the team didn't have anyone who carried a dominant presence with them. I am excluding Grant from that; he was the exception to that, but the rest of the team didn't have a dominant presence. I knew early on two things that I wanted: somebody or a couple of players with a dominant presence on the floor, either offensively or defensively. I wanted guys who could make plays. If you go back and look at our roster in 1999 they were good complementary players, but other people had to make plays to get Lindsey a shot or to get Christian a shot. If you look at that roster all the guys needed someone to make the play for them, and if Grant didn't make the play then it was tough for everybody else. I said we needed more than one guy who can make a play. Those were the two things: people who could make plays and people who had a presence on the court.

"We caught the break of a lifetime by getting 6'9" Ben Wallace. There's only two or three other seven-footers in the league that are more dominant then Ben around the basket in terms of presence: Shaquille O'Neal, Tim Duncan, and maybe Kevin Garnett. He's one of the top five dominant players around that lane in the league. So we caught the break of a lifetime to have a 6'9" guy who changed the complexion of who we were."

Getting Something from the Loss of Hill

Losing Grant Hill to free agency could have been a devastating blow to the team, but Dumars used a sign-and-trade agreement to get something of value in return.

"I took over as president of basketball operations in June of 2000 and two weeks later Grant Hill walked into my office and said he decided he was going to play in Orlando. So instead of just going, he gave me the option of making a sign and trade. I began watching films of their games and watched Ben Wallace getting eight/nine rebounds a game in 20 minutes, and I'm thinking 'Man, how many rebounds would he get if he was playing 35 minutes a game?' And I knew Chucky Atkins would help us at point guard. That got things rolling.

"I do know when I introduced Ben to Detroit, I said to people right then that he's a cross between Rick Mahorn and Dennis Rodman. I said Mahorn because of his physical play around the basket and the fact that he's not going to be pushed around or bullied around the lane, and Dennis Rodman because of his incredible athleticism and being able to rebound, shot-block and run and do all those things. He's held true to that and even surpassed that. I guess my favorite line is I thought he'd be good; I didn't know he'd be great.

"Ben forces his teammates to play at his level without ever saying a word. That's leadership to me. There's a rah-rah and yelling at players, but that doesn't always work. The leadership that always works is laying it on the line every night until it forces everybody to play at that high level. His energy and tenacity on the court is just as infectious to our team.

"When you're in this business, you can be good at it, but you better be lucky somewhere down the line. You just can't be, 'Oh, I'm so good at this job.' It pays to be good, but you have to catch a lucky break sometime, and we caught the break of a lifetime with this guy. We went from being a soft team that nobody really gave a second thought, to if you drive that lane, you're looking for Ben Wallace. Before we made the deal with Orlando, I started watching tape. I watched about six games. I just watched him and watched him and watched him. Then I looked at his stats. He was getting almost nine rebounds a game in just 20 minutes per game. I'm watching him on tape and I'm looking at his numbers and I'm saying if this guy were playing 30 minutes a game he'd probably average 10 to 12 rebounds per game and block a couple of shots. That's what I expected. I didn't have anything else to go on but what I saw. He was playing hard, he was relentless and he was only playing 20 minutes a game. I'd love to sit here and tell you I'd knew he'd be this good, but I didn't."

Adding the Next Pieces

While getting a rebounding machine like Wallace and Atkins, an excellent guard, was a great start to the rebuilding process, Dumars needed more pieces. Ironically, he turned to a team run by a former rival from the Pistons-Celtics days.

"It's been a slow process from that point on trying to add more size to the team. I went back and watched a lot of tape on Chauncey Billups. I always liked him. I tried to trade for him a year earlier with Minnesota. I talked to Kevin McHale about five times. The first four times I tried to convince him to trade Chauncey to me. The fifth time he said, 'Joe, I'm not going to trade Chauncey to you; let's talk about something else.' He just finally told me not to call about Chauncey anymore. The reason I wanted him was at that particular time I was looking at the Eastern Conference, and I said you need size if you're going to compete at the point guard spot in the East... Andre Miller had just come off a huge year for Cleveland. He had size, strength; he was a big point guard. Kenny Anderson had hurt us in the playoffs with his size at 6'2" or 6'3". You had Baron Davis who was coming on. You just knew this kid was going to be real good.

"I sat there and said you can't compete, as much as I loved Chucky Atkins, with a 5'9", 5'10" point guard against these guys. If you're going to compete with these point guards you're going to have to have some size and talent. What I saw in Chauncey was a guy who could make shots, is athletic, can make plays, but people had never gave him the chance to just play one position. People always tried to make him a point and a two [shooting guard]. That's okay, but early on in his career I think that hurt him, not having one position. I don't think he really had a chance to lock in. Now, I think he can play the one and the two. He can make that transition during the course of a game. He came out of school after his sophomore year, and it's hard for a kid 19 or 20 to play two different positions and ask him to play them great. So I said we'd bring him here and just make him a point guard. Just play point guard for us and not worry about anything else. Just show me you can compete against these other big point guards. The guy was the No. 3 pick in the draft, and it was just a hunch. I thought he could play. I played against him when he was a rookie and remembered that he was pretty strong. I remember banging with him a little bit. He was big, he was strong and he was athletic. People had kind of given up on him at different times. I just kind of put my arms around him and tried to make this kid a point guard because I thought he had the ability to do that."

Keeping Talent

When Chauncey came aboard he said he had been a fan of Dumars growing up, and that helped in the recruitment process when the Pistons signed him as a free agent.

"The idolization thing with Chauncey was secondary," said Dumars. "You can idolize somebody, but if they're in a terrible situation, I don't think that'll bring you there. I think Chauncey came because we had won the season before.

Increasing the talent and depth of the roster with players like Tayshaun Prince sold the Pistons' winning attitude to veteran players as well. (AP/WWP)

"When I initially talked to him, that's what appealed to him. 'You guys are winning. You guys are headed in the right direction. You guys have a chance. I like where you guys are going and I'd like to be a part of that, and, oh by the way, I've always idolized you.'

"I think the fact that we were winning and that we had turned the corner, I think that sold us more than anything.

"It sold us with other guys as well. It sold us with Richard Hamilton wanting to come back here and re-signing. It sold us with Elden Campbell, saying Indiana is after me, San Antonio is after me, Sacramento was after me before they made their deals; Philly, Miami. Eight or nine teams were after that guy. He saw what we were doing here and he said I want to be a part of that.

"Winning sells that for you. I can talk all day, I can make sense, I can be honest, I can make all the sense in the world, but you've got to win, man.

"We don't need stars. We need guys who want to do what it takes to win, and a lot of times that means giving up your own stats to get the W."

Big Ben

Wallace became the staple of the franchise. With the mottos "Hard Work" and "Goin' to Work," the community embraced Wallace, the strong silent type who let his work on the court speak for him.

Undrafted out of Virginia Union after transferring from Cuyahoga Community College in Cleveland, where they call him "Tri-C," Wallace spent his first season with the Washington Bullets as a free agent and played in just 34 games in 1996-97. The following year he started 16 of the 67 games he played and 16 of the 46 in 1998-99.

The following year he was acquired by Orlando from Washington along with Terry Davis, Tim Legler, and Jeff McInnis for Ike Austin. Wallace played a season in Orlando. Late in the year he played with a wrist so bad that he needed surgery after the season and an ankle that most players wouldn't have been able to walk on, let alone play on. But Wallace missed just one game while grabbing 665 rebounds and blocking 130 shots playing 24 minutes per game.

Where Does Superman Get His Energy?

Try taking a trip to Richmond, Virginia, in the summer. That's where Wallace works out, at Barco-Stevens Gymnasium. During the summer they call it the Hot Box because there's no air conditioning and few windows with tin walls. There's a sign on the wall that says "When you play, play hard. When you work, don't play at all."

Ben spends a lot of his time in The Cage, a small chain-link fenced area where there are rusted free weights and vinyl benches. On a typical summer's day, Wallace will do 200-pound curls and 150-pound triceps presses and get up to 460 pounds on the bench press. On other days, he'll do burnouts; he'll put 50 pounds on the curl bar, do one rep and put it down, do two reps and put it down until he gets all the way up to 20. He'll follow that up by getting out on the court for sprints and rebounding drills. Finally, with the temperature inside hovering around 100, he'll play with the likes of his mentor, Charles Oakley, Johnny Newman, Terry Davis, etc.

"It's a man's game," said Wallace. "Young guys can't play. We play too hard for them. They like to stand out there and pat the ball and look pretty. We play basketball."

A True Role Model

Wallace was the 10th of Sadie Wallace's 11 children, and they grew up in a three-bedroom house. He was born in Whitehall, Alabama, and grew up in Benton, 15 miles outside of Selma.

Sadie picked cotton with her husband to support the family. She made their clothes, and Ben spent time in the fields picking crops.

"Everything our mom did taught us from her life experiences," said Wallace. "The way she did things was the way I thought everybody did them. It was like I was blind to the real struggle. I just remember being happy."

His happiness became sheer joy when the Pistons traded for him and signed him to a six-year, $30 million deal. He immediately became the team's starting power forward, although he was listed as a center on the All-Star ballot.

His first year he started and played in 80 games and averaged 6.4 points, 13.4 rebounds and 2.33 blocked shots. He finished tied for fifth for Defensive Player of the Year honors, and his ferocious blocks and dunks became commonplace at the Palace.

The following year he appeared in 80 games again and averaged a career-best 7.6 points, led the league with 13 rebounds and blocked shots at a rate of 3.48 per game. He was named the league's Defensive Player of the Year and made third-team All-NBA.

Not resting on his laurels, Wallace went to work again in 2002-2003, averaging 15.4 rebounds to lead the league, the most by a Piston since Dennis Rodman in 1992-93. He was second in blocked shots at 3.06 and tacked on 1.42 steals. He tied or set franchise records for rebounds in a quarter (13), rebounds in a half (17), free throws attempted in a quarter (9), half (12) and a game (22), steals (7), offensive rebounds (11), defensive rebounds in a quarter (9), half (12) and game (17).

"He means everything to us," said Chauncey Billups. "He's the best rebounder in the league. He's a great teammate.

He's an All-Star and we feed off him. We wouldn't be where we are at without him."

This past season Wallace became just the second player to reach 100 blocks and 100 steals in four straight seasons. Hakeem Olajuwon was the other.

"That's a good stat," said Larry Brown. "I've seen a lot of guys get steals when they gamble on defense, but I don't think Ben gets involved where he's gambling on defense and putting the team at risk. That makes it even more impressive."

"He's similar to Rodman," said Mahorn. "He gets there at the right time and works hard to get it. He's similar to Rodman in strength and endurance. He's very unselfish and a very hard worker. You've got to love a guy who is very low-maintenance and doesn't ask for the basketball. What makes him special is he never takes a night off.

"He was the MVP of the team again, by far. Scoring takes all headlines and that's all well and good, but when you look at the character of your team, without Ben we wouldn't have been where we were. Defensively, day in and day out, he keeps giving you an average of three blocks a game and 15 rebounds and his interior play speaks for itself. These guys need extra rebounds, and Ben was the guy who went out and got them."

A Tough All-Star Appearance

Wallace made his first All-Star appearance two years ago in Atlanta, but it was bittersweet. That week, on February 1 while he was hawking the New Jersey Nets with seven blocked shots in the first half, Sadie Wallace fell unconscious in a grocery store

Ben Wallace was a great pickup from the Grant Hill sign-and-trade, and he led the Pistons to the 2004 NBA championship. (AP/WWP)

near Selma. Ben left the game and arena at halftime, but his mother died before he reached home.

The Saturday before the All-Star game he buried his mother at a service in Selma. He was about to become the first All-Star player who wasn't drafted, and his mom wasn't there to see him. Nearly 1,500 people attended the funeral, including Dumars and Michael Curry, while his brother, Rev. James Wallace, presided over the service.

"It had always been a goal of mine to make the All-Star team," Wallace said hours before participating in the game. "But to be in the starting lineup and have my name announced is something I never dreamed about. I don't know how I'll react when they say my name. It's the result of a lot of hard work and effort paying off, considering where I came from."

Continued Excellence

Proving it was no fluke, Wallace was the Eastern Conference's top vote-getter at center and started for the second straight year in Los Angeles. It was a better setting than the previous year when he was a day away from his mother's funeral.

"I couldn't really enjoy it the first time because I had other things going on," said Wallace. "Getting there the first time, people could say it was a fluke. The second time...That's a different story. It's one thing to be considered an All-Star, but to be voted in by the fans, especially nowadays when people say fans just come to see offense and guys dunking and all that. It means a lot."

Wallacemania has spread throughout the country. It's commonplace to walk into an opposing arena and see a kid or adult, white or black, wearing an Afro wig and the Pistons' No. 3.

"It's a big surprise," declared Wallace. "I never thought it would get to this point. I've seen it happen for a lot of other guys, but I never thought it would happen to me. To be on the road and see people wearing the Afro and screaming at me to take the cornrows down and let the 'Fro out...It's just a great feeling for me right now. I have a sense now that I do belong here on this team and the community has taken to me like a second son."

This past season he had to play Game 3 of the Eastern Conference semifinals against New Jersey on Mother's Day. It was an emotional time, but Wallace was the only Piston who played well with a career-playoff-high 24 rebounds and 15 points. After the game Wallace sat in front of his locker with a towel over his face.

"I knew this was going to be a tough weekend," said Wallace. "Playing on Mother's Day knowing the situation with my mom...I knew it wasn't going to be easy. Losing a game you can bounce back from, but knowing I'd never be able to see her again..."

Picking Up Cliff

Another key frontcourt contributor that Dumars added to the team was Cliff Robinson.

"When I traded Jud Buechler and John Wallace for Cliff Robinson, he gave us versatility up front. He was just what we needed to go along with Ben. Ben is what he is around that basket, but you're not going to get the versatility of a Cliff

While Cliff Robinson was a valuable member of the team in 2003, he couldn't help the Pistons get past the Nets in the Eastern Conference Finals. (AP/WWP)

Robinson, who can guard a three [small forward], who can guard a four [power forward], who can guard a five. I looked at Cliff one time during the season and I remember he guarded [Tracy] McGrady in Orlando. He guarded Rasheed Wallace at the four spot and Kenyon Martin at the four spot and Karl Malone at the four spot. And I saw him try to wrestle with Shaq a little bit. That's not to say he shut any of those guys down, but the ability to put a guy on each one of those three different positions is a luxury most teams didn't have."

To Chuck Daly, it was yet another deal to bring the Pistons back to the elite of the NBA.

"Joe has done a great job with all the deals he's made, and he's put the city back behind them. It's a perfect mix of a working man's town and the working man's team."

Trading Jerry

One of the more difficult decisions Dumars had to make was trading local favorite Jerry Stackhouse. He just felt that Richard Hamilton would fit better with what the team was trying to accomplish.

"From a pure basketball standpoint, I thought Rip and Jerry were both 20-point-plus-a-night guys, but I thought the fashion in which Rip got his 20 points a night fit more with what we were trying to do here. Stack's my guy, I love Stack, but Stack has to dominate the ball to be effective on the court. Rip doesn't have to. Rip is in constant motion. He can come off screens and shoot, so you can run never lose your chemistry or continuity on the floor with Rip out there. With Stack, everybody has to stop and let him do his thing and hopefully he can carry you. With Rip you don't have to slow up with him; keep doing everything you're doing and he'll find his way to get his.

"From a pure basketball standpoint, I looked at it and said to keep the continuity and direction we're going in he's going to be a better fit.

"I'm more critical of guards, as I am sure Kevin McHale is more critical of big guys. I'm sure Larry Bird may be more critical of the small forward spot. You're more critical of the position that you played because you know it so well and you know what a guy should or shouldn't be doing at that position. I'm more critical of the guard position and I expect a lot out of them. So picking up those two young guys, Chauncey and Rip, as a backcourt, I'm not in their ear a lot, but after certain games I'll pull Chauncey aside or I'll pull Rip aside and go over about three or four different things they did that night. OK, in the third quarter with 6:22 left you made this play. What were you thinking? Things like that."

Rip

Hamilton came to the Pistons with a reputation as a mid-range scorer who wasn't a strong three-point shooter, but could run all day and bury his defender in a myriad of screens and picks set by bigger teammates.

Hamilton was listed at 6'7" and 193 pounds, but he seemed slimmer. His endurance was questioned, but he showed early that he had a lot of heart and that his most outstanding player award in the 1999 NCAA championship was earned.

"Rip" averaged 19.7 points per game to lead the team in scoring his first year. It was a far cry from Stackhouse's average of 29.8 points per game in 2000-2001, but the Pistons were trying to diversify the offense and not just rely on one player.

Hamilton's play was even better in the playoffs as the Pistons reached the Eastern Conference Finals. For the 17 playoff games, he averaged 22.5 points per game, shot 44.2 percent from the field and 33.3 percent from three-point land. One of the league's best free throw shooters, Hamilton averaged 83.3 during the regular season and 90.6 in the playoffs.

During the offseason, Hamilton became the richest Piston in team history, signing a seven-year deal that was to pay him $63 million.

"I had nothing when I was growing up," said Hamilton "and I mean nothing. Nobody ever makes it out of Coatesville [Pennsylvania]. I never got to meet anybody famous; no celebrities ever came to see us. I made a promise that if I ever got out of Coatesville and made something of myself that I was going to do everything I could to help people no matter where I lived."

Coatesville was a town of 11,000 in southeast Pennsylvania. Detroit was a town just under a million people with a heritage of embracing its sports stars.

Sharing His Good Fortune

Last Thanksgiving, Hamilton, in his second year, and some teammates helped donate 900 turkeys to the Capuchin Soup Kitchen. He showed up to shake hands with the people and spread some holiday cheer.

In the summer he sponsors an annual daylong event called "Rip City Celebration" in Coatesville. Kids and adults enjoy swimming, arts and crafts, basketball, reading, and musical performances. Hamilton pays for everything himself.

"I have more fun than anybody," said the former Connecticut All-American. "I give away bikes, toys, games, T-shirts, food. I just throw a party for everybody. I want people to come up to me and be able to say 'Yo, what's up, Rip?' and not be afraid. I'm still one of them."

When Stackhouse was traded, Hamilton became the team's captain of the NBA's Read to Achieve program. The role takes him to Detroit and Flint schools where he reads to kids and makes an impact on kids aspiring to "make it."

A news story said he had a particular impact on Detroit's Damon Keith Elementary, where the school posted a 9.3 MEAP reading rating among fourth graders in 2002, meaning that 90.7 percent of the kids who took the test did not meet its standards. The score jumped to 40.3 in 2003 with Hamilton receiving credit for inspiring the kids.

During the Pistons' run to the 2004 NBA championship, Hamilton proved tough and overcame a couple of demons, Indiana defensive ball-hawk Ron Artest and the Lakers' Kobe Bryant, a high school nemesis back in Pennsylvania.

Hamilton could easily have been the MVP of the playoffs. He averaged 21.5 points in 23 playoff games and shot 44.7 percent from the field to go with 4.6 rebounds and 4.2 assists per game. His 33 points against Inidana in Game 5 helped the Pistons claim a road win and his 31 points in Game 3 against the Lakers led a 20-point blowout.

It was his time.

"The whole experience was unbelievable," said Hamilton. "It was what I thought and more."

Chapter

FOREIGN IMPORTS

The Globalization of the NBA

Joe Dumars faces a very different talent pool than when he was drafted into the league.

"I think when I was in high school and college and very early in my pro career it was always referred to as the NBA college draft. By the time my career ended I realized that it wasn't the NBA college draft any more. They should call it the NBA worldwide draft, because by no means are you just drafting college kids any more. That's a term that's so outdated that it's almost a joke. It's the high school draft, the junior college draft, the college draft, it's the European draft, it is the worldwide draft now."

*For president of basketball operations Joe Dumars, acquiring talent for
the organization has become far more complicated than in his playing
days. (AP/WWP)*

Dipping into International Waters

According to Dumars, it made sense from a talent and business sense to expand the franchise's search for players outside the United States.

"I just felt that we as an organization were behind the times in terms of looking at the world as a resource. The whole world is a resource now, so why would you just look at a portion of it? It's a global world now in every sense. In the media business, guess what? They can read your articles from here to China. If you think you're writing and it's only going to be digested by those in your community you're crazy. People read your stuff all over the world.

"We had to open our eyes and take the blinders off and become a more global-thinking organization. That's what I set out to do immediately."

Adding an Expert

In order to expand their borders, Dumars needed an expert. He believes that he found one.

"Tony Ronzone is the director of international scouting, and I say unashamedly that he's the best in the business. He's the best at what he does. He's universally known as the best. He had tremendous resources around the world. I mean tremendous. You hear someone tell you that when they're trying to sell themselves, and when I sat Tony down, I said talk to me about your contacts, and he tells me I'm in good with this federation and I know these people. I've been to Europe with him, I've been to Belgrade, Yugoslavia, with him, I've been to South America with him, I've been to Stockholm, Sweden, with him. You see him and you get there with him and you see these people greeting him like he's the royal family. They are meeting and greeting him and almost bowing to him because he was over there when it wasn't fashionable to be over there. He was over there 10 years ago when the only people in the NBA from over there at that time were [Drazen] Petrovic and [Vlade] Divac was maybe just getting over here. He was there, full blown, all the way. Those people love him over there, so it gave us inroads over there that I can probably say nobody else has. You can ask a lot of people across the league and they'll tell you that Tony's the best and there are a whole lot of other people second.

"My thing was if we were going to go internationally let's try and get the best people in the world. I feel like we've gotten that with Tony. He was with the Dallas Mavericks at the time and Mark Cuban had a different vision of how he wanted to run his international operation. He wanted to hire a local person in each one of those countries. He wanted to get a coach who had been coaching in Italy for years and make him the guy in that part of the country that he'd call and make inroads. He did that in France, he did that in Germany. He did that with different people around the world, which is a completely different strategy in terms of putting your international thing together. When he did that it basically took the legs from underneath Tony. Before he did that Tony was his contact with each one of those countries. It took a lot of the responsibility away from Tony and it really left him being underutilized, and they knew it. They also knew he was great. When I called down and talked to Cuban and talked to Don Nelson, they understood that they weren't utilizing him at his best, but this is the way we wanted to do it. They said, 'Joe, if you're looking to set it up the way we originally had it set up with Tony, this is your guy.' I said absolutely. I said I need him, I want him. The timing was perfect. If I had gone after him a year earlier, he was the point person for all these things. The great thing about it was when he came to Detroit he continued to have all those relationships. He sat in my office and called every one of those countries and said I'm a Detroit Piston now, but I'm still your guy. It's my relationship with you that is the most important thing. He goes in with his Pistons hats and golf shirts and T-shirts and takes care of all his friends over there, and they welcome us with open arms.

"Tony is in and out representing the NBA. He's in and out and he's not going to make a lot of enemies. He always seems like he's just arriving or just about to leave. That's who he has been for the last 10 to 15 years. That has been his lifestyle, and often you don't know whether he's coming or going. He has embraced that lifestyle, and that's why from Jerry West to Donnie Walsh to Rod Thorn they'll tell you that guy is the best, and Detroit was lucky."

Mehmet Okur

The addition of Ronzone began paying immediate dividends for the Pistons, starting with a big man from Turkey.

"The morning of the day we drafted Mehmet Okur, Tony brought him in about 10 o'clock. We worked him out until 11. He walked out and bought Mehmet a suit at The Rochester Big and Tall Store, put him on a plane, went back to New York and got him back in time for the draft.

"He went out and sat with the fans in the stands, and when we came up at 38 he was still on the board. We grabbed him right away. That's one of those things. At that particular time we were talking about Jarron Collins at 38: 6'11", big body. Everybody was sitting in the draft room, and I had just hired Tony three days before the draft. The meeting ended and everybody walked out, and Tony knocked on the door and came back in. Tony said, 'I don't want to step on anybody's toes and say something that wouldn't be received well.' He said, 'I have two kids who are better than Jarron Collins. If either one of them is there at 38 I would recommend that you take either one of these kids. I said OK, how can I see them and how will I know that? He said they both were in the United States. They both had just worked out for Memphis. He said he could call because they were getting ready to go back to New York and sit around for the draft. He said he could get them in here for tomorrow morning, the day of the draft. I said, 'Make it happen,' so he got on the phone, mades some calls and said they'll be here at nine in the morning and be ready to work out at 10.

"They came in and worked out. I looked at Tony and said yeah. Right away I knew Mehmet wouldn't be there at 38 because he was that good, so I said we'd look at the other kid. Lo and behold, that's how we got Mehmet Okur, because otherwise I wouldn't have known who he was. When Mehmet Okur and Ratko Varda walked in here, I didn't know who was Mehmet and who was Ratko. I had never seen them, I had never heard of them. That's what a guy like Tony brings you."

Unfortunately the Pistons won't see Okur's development firsthand. Brown wasn't big on seven-footers who are able to shoot three-pointers. Okur struggled early and often under Brown's system. It didn't mean he couldn't play; it was just difficult for Okur and Brown to reach a mutual understanding of his role.

A restricted free agent over the summer of 2004, Okur was offered a six-year, $50 million deal the Pistons were unable to match. Knowing they'd lose Okur, Dumars picked up free agent forward Antonio McDyess, plagued by knee and ankle problems the last three years. More of an inside player, McDyess, if healthy, could be a tremendous pickup and help soften the blow of the loss of Okur.

Zeljko Rebraca

Okur was not the only international player the Pistons added quickly after the decision to commit to the global game. With Dumars' understanding that Okur would not come right in and make an immediate impact on the roster, he went looking for some additional depth.

"That same summer I told him that was great size we just added, but that kid's not going to be able to come over this year," Dumars said of Okur. "I said is anybody else in Europe? He said yeah, but somebody else has his rights. He said Zeljko Rebraca. He has been a great center over in Europe for years and he's about 29 years old. I told him to get tapes. He got on the phone and called Europe, said he needed to FedEx some tapes overnight, and the next morning they're here. I watched about three of his games and asked him who has his rights. He said Toronto. I talked to Glen Grunwald, and he said he didn't want to do it right away. Then he said he'd take a first-round pick for him because he's that good. He said he's better than any of the young centers you are going to draft. I said I'm not going to give you a first-round pick. You drafted him in the second round; he hasn't played over here. I will give you a second-round pick. We ended up doing it for a second-round pick. I'm a little biased towards Rebraca because I don't know if he has really gotten a fair chance to prove how really good he could be over here. It has always been a little salt in the water. I'm looking forward to seeing how he does in a different circumstance, and he's healthy now.

"Once again, if not for Tony Ronzone sitting in my office, Mehmet Okur would not be a Piston, Zeljko Rebraca's not here, Pepe Sanchez probably isn't here. We knew who Pepe Sanchez was, but it was Tony who knew the people in Argentina. He knew Pepe's contacts and I didn't. This was two years ago that we drafted Mehmet Okur, and it was two years ago that he told me that there were some great young kids coming out of Europe. He said there's a kid over there 16 and I'd draft him right now. He said Darko Milicic. He said remember that name. Tony told me about this kid two years ago. He said, 'Joe, we won't have a chance to get this kid because he'll be a top five pick.' I said we might have a chance, we've got that Memphis pick sitting out there, if we ever got lucky. He said, 'If we ever got that lucky we'd be on cloud nine.' Lo and behold two years later what happens? The ball pops up with the second pick and we get Darko."

Winning the Second Pick in the Lottery

The draft lottery is a process that is supposed to help the poor teams get the best talent. A squad like the Pistons, coming off consecutive 50-win seasons, had no business competing for the first pick in the draft. But years earlier, the Pistons had traded Otis Thorpe to the Vancouver/Memphis Grizzlies for a future number one pick. In 2003, when the Pistons exercised the pick, (it was only protected for Memphis if it was the number one pick) Memphis was in the draft lottery, so the team had a shot at a top talent in a rich draft that also included LeBron James, Carmelo Anthony, Dwayne Wade, Chris Bosh, and the talented European Ronzone had mentioned to Dumars years earlier.

This is how I look at the lottery night," said Dumars. "We had done everything we were supposed to do up until that point. We were sitting there in the conference finals. We had executed everything in our power to get to that night. Then the ball falls in place for us. That's why I'm talking about the planning and the vision. Up until that point everything had worked beautifully until that night. Now, we get the break of a lifetime and get the No. 2 pick. When the chance came to get the break of a lifetime, we had prepared to take advantage of that break. There were some teams that could've gotten the No. 2 pick and they would've still been way back here. We got the breaks that every team needs, but we also did the preparation by getting to the conference finals. We're probably one of the few teams that have gotten the No. 2 pick and can honestly say we're not counting on that player to save us. If you're picking No. 2 you need that guy to play 25 to 30 minutes a night and play big for you. We don't need that."

Finding a Lucky Charm

For Dumars, every little superstition that could help him win the lottery was appreciated, even a tiny piece of copper:

"I was coming out of my room and saw a penny on the floor. It was a penny from 1989, and I kept that penny because 1989 was a good year for this organization. I still have that

Winning the second pick in the 2003 NBA draft lottery allowed the Pistons to add Darko Milicic. (AP/WWP)

penny. Down in Louisiana they tell you if you see a penny, pick it up, baby. I grew up with that. I picked it up, and I'm walking to my room and I'm saying 1989; this is the day of the lottery and I'm saying you know what? 1989 was a good year. We won the championship. I got the MVP in the finals. I said, 'Maybe this is going to be some good luck.'"

Carlos Delfino

For Detroit, the international hit list continued.

The team managed to get Delfino with the 25th pick in the 2003 draft. He did not play that first season on Detroit's championship team, instead playing in Italy. However, Dumars and the rest of the organization expect him to be a key contributor soon, particularly after his role on Argentina's gold medal-winning Olympic squad.

Convincing the Coach

Detroit's foreign imports haven't immediately made a splash with Brown.

Okur, in the last year of his deal in 2003-2004 and a restricted free agent over the summer of 2004, started the season on the bench as Elden Campbell won the starting center's job in training camp. A great outside shooter, Okur would often find himself being yanked if he didn't get under the basket and post up. At times during the season it became a problem when the big center-forward from Turkey would draw Brown's ire for settling on a jump shot instead of working his way into the post for an easier shot, such as a five-footer or layup.

One night in Cleveland after a timeout in which Okur was instructed by Brown to post up and try to score, Brown took exception with Okur when he launched a jump shot instead.

After the game, Brown publicly scolded Okur and said if there was any miscommunication about the play, it got more than cleared up after Okur took the shot. It was Brown's way of getting Okur to play the right way, and often during the season you could hear Brown shouting Okur's name in reference to a blown defensive assignment or bad field goal attempt.

For his part, Okur kept a positive attitude despite the ups and downs with his new coach. While Carlisle let him shoot threes the season before, Brown was more demanding, and his up-and-down minutes reflected his struggles. Defensively, Okur would let his man squeeze past him for offensive rebounds or he would rotate too much to help a beaten teammate. These were all problems that he had to iron out if he expected more playing time.

"I want to go out there and make things happen," Okur said. "I have learned very much watching the other players. I didn't know some of the rules and changes getting into the NBA when I first got here. I was used to playing international basketball. My teammates and coaches stop me when I have done something wrong in practice and show me what I should be doing instead."

He admitted after he signed with Utah that the year, despite winning the championship, was taxing on him.

Turning the Corner

Dumars was closely watching, and so were his teammates, who realized that Okur's game could help them reach the NBA Finals if he "played the right way."

Okur had his moments.

On November 7 against Milwaukee he had a career-high 18 rebounds, eight offensive, to help the Pistons to a home victory despite shooting just three of 11 from the field.

On November 23 he was at it again, grabbing eight offensive boards and 18 total in a home loss to New Orleans. Again, Okur shot poorly from the field, making just three of 12 field goal attempts.

"I feel OK, not so bad," Okur said during one bad stretch. "Sometimes I fight myself in the game. I'll miss a rebound or a shot, and I just fight myself. I think I'm doing better every day. There's not pressure on me. I just try to do something right way when I get in. It's not happening sometimes, but I'm getting better. It's not my teammates or the plays. I work hard to do my job out there, and I'm ready to go. I like playing inside and outside. This year it's much different. Larry Brown wants us first to run inside, and if you catch the ball inside, just play. It's not just play outside and do whatever you want to do. I'm cool with that, and I try to push myself this way. I'll be fine."

His most complete game may have come on January 14 against Toronto. Ben Wallace got thrown out of the game and Okur came to the rescue, scoring 27 points and pulling down 14 rebounds in a 95-91 victory.

Okur started 33 of the 71 games he played and averaged 9.6 points and 5.9 rebounds during the regular season, both career highs.

"I was on him about rebounding the ball and working hard defensively and trying to post up a little bit more," said Brown. "He has done that. People have to remember that he and Tayshaun didn't play major minutes last year. It's early for them. They're going to have ups and downs."

The Other Side of the Coin

While Okur experienced both ups and downs, Rebraca experienced mostly downs.

Much was expected of the big center from Serbia and Montenegro. In the 2002-2003 season, an irregular heartbeat had sidelined him from late December to just before the start of the playoffs. Injuries and uncertainty about his role always shadowed Rebraca, who was a hero in his country.

Over the following summer he had surgery to correct the problem, and in late September seemed ready to come back and make a contribution to the team.

"It has not been easy," Rebraca said before he was traded. "I want to play. I want to help. I have been trying to get healthy again. It took longer than I thought. I do not have the same feel, the same flow of the game that I had before. I need to play more. I need to practice more than to come back. I need time. The fans have been very good to me. I appreciate all of their nice wishes for me. I want to do well for them."

He started out sluggish, and at one point in the season Brown referred to Rebraca as a player performing like he was on his deathbed. The comment bothered Rebraca, who was fighting for playing time behind Okur and Elden Campbell.

Methodical at times, he played in just 21 games during the season with two starts. He averaged just 3.1 points and 2.3 rebounds per game. For a player in the last year of his contract, he wasn't winning over Dumars or the coaching staff.

Finally, he was traded along with Bobby Sura to Atlanta, thus ending his Pistons career on a down note.

The Rookie

While Rebraca was a disappointment, Milicic was a source of public scrutiny on a daily basis during the season. Because he was sandwiched between two of the greatest 19-year-olds ever to play in the league—LeBron James and Carmelo Anthony—his first year in Detroit was played, or rather not played, under a magnifying glass.

James has been used to the spotlight since his sophomore year in high school at St. Vincent-St. Mary's in Akron. Anthony led Syracuse to the NCAA championship as a freshman, then bolted for the NBA. Both made the Olympic Team after all the defections.

Milicic hardly played for his Hemofarm Vrsac team, and coming over from Serbia and Montenegro, he not only had to learn a new culture, but how to play under a Hall of Fame coach who wasn't going to let him take any shortcuts.

The 7'1", 253-pound Milicic impressed in a workout at John Jay College with his speed and athletic ability, but as far as basketball knowledge he was raw. When he worked out at the Palace, the Pistons had a press conference. Milicic announced that his mom was 6'3" and his dad 6'7".

He said in Europe when a team lost, fans would throw chairs and start fighting. Players wouldn't talk to each other for days, but he found the situation different in the States.

"There's no need to rush him and mess with his confidence," said Brown. "We want his experience to be a positive one. As an organization we don't feel there's any need to throw him out there."

Despite the clamoring from fans, Brown and his staff didn't throw Milicic out there. Ignoring the success of James and Anthony, the Pistons stuck to the plan, playing their teenager occasionally while he learned the ropes.

"Before the draft you wouldn't have found one team that would have taken Milicic over Anthony," said Dumars. "I was under the microscope 14 years as a player so I can deal with the criticism. I thought, in my heart of hearts, this was the right thing for us. So I did it."

The world watched and Milicic sat.

When he wasn't giddy about playing a minute or two at the end of games, Brown publicly scolded him.

"I do think I'm hard on Darko and Mehmet because they're young and developing, and I don't think they really know what it takes to succeed based on the ability they have. I think it's important for me to push them.

"Joe never forced me to play Darko this year, and I don't think the plan was to play him. We have a veteran team, and he has time to learn. It would be different if he were in Cleveland or Denver. He'd have to play. I think we have to protect Darko, period. He's a foreign kid. He's younger than anybody else. He should be a senior in high school. He's coming on a winning team. There's going to be a lot of things that are going to be different from LeBron and Carmelo.

"Darko's coming along. He's very athletic and runs the floor. You can see in practice that he's getting better every day. He has to learn that every second he plays is important."

Brown thought it was unfair to Milicic that when he played at home fans expected him to score every time he touched the ball.

If the Pistons had a big lead heading into the fourth quarter, fans would start shouting, "We want Darko, we want Darko."

Oftentimes Brown relented and let the rookie go in.

His jump shot would usually come up short. He'd try to dunk and be blocked by the rim. He rushed things instead of just playing in the framework of the team. Brown wanted Milicic to learn the low-post game before wandering outside for jump shots. The more he paid attention, the more he got to play later in the year.

"I'm more confident when I go in now, and Coach tells me to go down low," said Milicic.

His teammates sympathized with Milicic's plight.

"As a rookie coming in, especially one as young as Darko is, you have to earn the respect and trust of the coach," said former teammate Bobby Sura. "It's not easy in this league. A lot of coaches don't like the young guys coming in and playing a lot of minutes. You have to earn that. Down the road, it can make you a better player because of it. You just can't come in and jack up shots to try to score points. You can turn the coach off real quick in those few minutes."

When the Pistons visited Sacramento in early November, Milicic got a chance to visit and have dinner with veteran center Vlade Divac, a national hero in Serbia and Montenegro.

"He's too young," said Divac. "Coming over here with a new style of basketball and new culture....I'm very familiar with it. I was 21 when I came over. It's harder for him because he's still a kid. I told him to be patient and work hard and listen to what people around him are telling him. Sometimes when you're 18 you think you know everything, but he's a great kid. He wants to learn, but you have to have patience around him because he's 18. He's going to get there. A lot of kids look up to what I did over here. We all have the same dream: to play basketball and become an NBA player. He's here now, so he has to take advantage of it."

Divac was asked if he thought he got through to Milicic with his talk.

"He's listening to what I'm saying, but at the same time I have kids at home and I know they have a mind of their own," he said.

By the Pistons' playoff drive, the organization said he had grown another three-quarters of an inch, gained strength and not only took the poundings from Ben Wallace, but gave some back.

"He's the future of the organization," said Ben, the team's core player. "You can see it coming. He's going to be a good player."

However, that didn't translate to more court time.

"It's like night and day," admitted Chauncey Billups. "He has come so far from the first day of training camp. It's just a matter of time."

Time that critics weren't giving Brown and Dumars.

With James and Anthony tearing the league up, and even Chris Bosh of Toronto and Dwyane Wade of Miami showing they had the potential to be All-Stars, Milicic sat, and sat and sat, seeing mop-up duty whenever the game called for it.

"If people will just be patient and give this kid time," said Dumars, "he's going to be something special. We might be one of the few teams in recent memory that actually didn't need the second pick to come in and be a savior. Darko is hungry. I've seen where he came from, and you talk about kids over there not having anything....He came from a place where they literally had nothing."

When Hall of Fame player Magic Johnson commented on a Pistons game in December for Fox Sports, he said: "I have to commend Joe. I can see why he drafted the big fella instead of Carmelo Anthony with Tayshaun Prince here. Tayshaun's a much better defensive player than Carmelo right now, and with this being his second year, he's only going to get better and better with his defensive capabilities and his ability to make three-pointers."

Alas, in the final minutes of the Pistons' Game 5-clinching victory over L.A., Kareem Rush whacked at Milicic's hand while grabbing a rebound and broke this thumb. Days after the Finals Milicic had surgery to repair the thumb, and the injury caused him to miss being a member of the Serbia and Montenegro National Team. The experience of playing on a national stage would've helped his maturation. Now, with the addition of Antonio McDyess and Derrick Coleman over the summer along with the broken thumb, it's difficult to tell how much progress Milicic will make over the summer.

Chapter 10

THE 2004 PLAYOFFS

Back to the Conference Finals

As the Pistons got ready for the 2004 playoffs, it was clear to Joe Dumars that he needed one more piece to get his team over the top. And eventually, he got that piece.

The Biggest Trade of the Year

Dumars had his eye on Rasheed Wallace for a while. He had heard the stories and seen the antics on the court with Rasheed, but knowing he was in the last year of his contract and that Portland likely had seen enough of the 6'11" power forward/center, the Pistons' president of basketball operations was willing to take a chance despite the reputation Wallace had on and off the court.

"Right before the season started, in training camp we talked to John Nash about it. At the time they were asking for a ton."

The ton was Ben Wallace and Richard Hamilton, which was not going to happen.

"The talks continued on through the season, every few weeks," said Dumars. "We got close to the trade deadline and we started talking again. We thought we had a three-way deal going for a while. It was on again, off again. It was on, and then it fell through the fourth time."

"I didn't have enough. I was a Hubert Davis contract away from having enough."

That was important because Davis had asked to be released about a month before the All-Star break and the team obliged. If he had still been under contract with the Pistons, they could've worked the deal without losing Chucky Atkins, a valuable point guard off the bench, or involving a third team.

Needing another club to help make the move work, Dumars found a taker for Atkins and Lindsey Hunter in Danny Ainge and the Boston Celtics. Ainge, Boston's GM, was trying to get his club out of the playoff race and into the lottery, so he was more than happy to get involved.

"Danny and I had talked a few days before," said Dumars. "We were playing New York in New York [February 17] and Isiah [Thomas] had taken over and we were standing in that little hallway watching the game and my cell phone rang. Isiah was standing there, and I saw it was Danny Ainge. I told him I was going to walk back into the tunnel, and I said 'What's happening?' He said do you want to do this deal? And I said yes. Absolutely. He said OK, we've got a deal, we'll do it in the morning.

"I walked back up, put the phone in my pocket and continued to watch the game. It was a lot of phone calls.

Shifting the Balance of Power

"Indiana or New Jersey, wherever he ended up, he was going to make a difference. I just thought with our style, I knew he was a versatile guy and could play three [small forward], four [power forward] or five [center], and defend those guys. I thought with his versatility he could be the guy that could help us get here."

The Pistons were 34-22 when they acquired Rasheed and went 20-6 after he arrived, as the team won 54 games and put itself in a position to beat Indy and New Jersey.

As the Pistons were being swept last year in the Eastern Conference finals, Dumars already was plotting ways to improve the team.

"If you remain with the status quo, you're not a true contender," said Dumars. "We were a good playoff team and we were going to be somebody in the first round, but we weren't good enough to win it. To sit there and be content with that...You're not doing your job. Not really. That's why you can't be content until you feel like you have a legitimate shot to win it or until you get to this stage. You do less tinkering with your team at that point; then it becomes finding and improving a specific area.

"A couple of years ago we were in the playoffs, but I was looking at three or four positions. I said we might have to move [Jerry] Stackhouse, I got to get a different point guard, I need somebody a little more versatile at the three, I need more help

Rasheed Wallace was a key addition to the Pistons' 2004 championship run. (AP/WWP)

up front. Now, I don't do that. I look and say we need help in this area right now."

Dumars had always wanted to bring in a player who had a little bit of an edge. He didn't want a team where everybody acted and reacted the same. In bringing in Wallace and having a coach like Brown, who also had North Carolina ties, he thought the mix would work. Plus, the Pistons' locker room was solid, and no one individual was going to change it.

Rasheed's Arrival

When Wallace arrived for his first game and first press conference on February 20, he donned a Tony Gonzalez Kansas City Chiefs jersey.

When asked why, Rasheed said, "Because they're the best team in football." When told they didn't win the Super Bowl, he replied, "So? They're still the best team in football."

His first game wasn't a memorable one against Minnesota. He got in early in the first quarter, but was informed by halftime that he and Mike James couldn't play because there was a paperwork problem with the league and none of the participants in the trade were eligible to play. The blunder cost the Pistons $200,000, but Rasheed turned out to be worth the price.

Rasheed didn't think it would be enough to come to practice at the Pistons' workout facility and say "Good morning, Coach Brown." Even LB—short for Larry Brown—wasn't really enough. So the newest Piston started calling Brown "Pound-for-Pound."

That was a term usually reserved for a boxer who was considered pound-for-pound the best in the world.

For Rasheed, it was homage to the coach he considered the best in the game.

Before the Pistons obtained Rasheed on February 19, Detroit didn't appear to be ready to challenge Indiana or New Jersey for supremacy in the Eastern Conference. Even though the team was 34-22 and had a 13-game winning streak during the season, it was apparent that they weren't good enough to beat either Indiana or New Jersey. Both teams had handled the Pistons pretty well during the regular season to that point, and the Pistons were unable to handle Kenyon Martin of New Jersey or Jermaine O'Neal of Indiana. It was the Pacers who ended the Pistons' winning streak at Conseco with an 81-69 victory.

Indiana won the Central Division title, ending the Pistons' two-year run, but the belief was the Pistons could compete with the Pacers when they met in the Eastern Conference finals.

Making the Path a Bit Smoother

Rick Mahorn saw what the addition of Rasheed Wallace would do for the Pistons, particularly in the playoffs when his talent would help the team get past the the better teams in the league:

"After they made the trade for Rasheed Wallace, you could tell they were looking to make that push to the Finals," said Mahorn. "Without Rasheed we would've gone to the Eastern Conference finals and lost to Indiana. We needed something to get us over the hump. They could've beaten them [Indiana], but it would've been more of a struggle. They would've worn themselves down before they got to the Finals. A seven-game series with Jersey and then a seven-game series with Indy would've worn themselves down when it came to the Lakers. Defensively, they took the individual responsibility to try and stop people man to man. Indiana's defense was great, but like we were in '89, we knew what to do defensively and that's what this team did. They showed a lot of heart and desire. They weren't settling for just being there in the Finals. They wanted the end result, and when they saw the light at the end of the tunnel they went for it. They went through some struggles during the season, but they learned. They'd go through a two-game or three-game losing streak and then they'd circle the wagons because they didn't want to feel that pain any more. We did it a different way."

Beating the Young Bucks

When the Milwaukee Bucks lost their last game of the season, they fell to the sixth seed in the East and became the Pistons' first-round opponent.

A hard-working group under first-year coach Terry Porter, the Bucks fielded an All-Star in Michael Redd and the high-flying Desmond Mason, a capable scorer and rebounder at small forward.

Game 1 went according to plan as the Pistons had six players in double figures and drilled the Bucks 108-82.

Detroit's starting front line, an advantage in the series, all posted double-doubles as Tayshaun Prince scored 14 and had 11 rebounds with four blocked shots, Rasheed Wallace had 17 points and 10 rebounds and Ben Wallace grabbed 14 boards while scoring 17.

Richard Hamilton led all scorers with 21 points.

Losing Home Court

In what became a familiar trend during the playoffs, the Pistons lost home-court advantage with a 92-88 setback in Game 2. Redd rebounded from an 11-point effort in Game 1 with 26 points in Game 2 while Toni Kukoc emerged from the bench and made seven of eight shots and scored 15 points. Brevin Knight also hurt the Pistons with 11 points, seven rebounds and five assists.

Closing Out Milwaukee

With the series shifting back to Milwaukee for Game 3, the Bucks thought they had gained the momentum in the series, but again the Pistons' entire starting five scored in double figures, as the team used a 32-point third quarter to pull out a 95-85 victory to reclaim home court in the series.

Pounding the ball in the paint in Game 4, the Pistons scored 50 inside and had two 20-point scorers in a 109-92 victory to seize control of the series at 3-1. Hamilton ran the Bucks' defenders silly, scoring 27 on 10 of 17 shooting from the field while Rasheed added 20 and nine rebounds. Prince also was in double figures again with 17 points on eight of 11 shooting.

Back at the Palace for Game 5, the Pistons twisted the screws defensively and pounded the Bucks 91-77 to clinch the series. If there was an MVP of the series, it was Prince, who for the series averaged 17.4 points per game, shot 59.3 percent from the field, and averaged 7.6 rebounds and 2.2 blocked shots.

"I couldn't be more proud of him," said Brown afterward.

*Ben Wallace and the rest of the Pistons' frontcourt helped them domi-
nate the Bucks in Round 1 of the NBA playoffs. (AP/WWP)*

"In the Milwaukee series Tayshaun was the best player,"
said Mahorn. "Milwaukee didn't have any kind of small forward
or anybody that could check him. A lot of people thought he
was the MVP of the series, but I thought it was more Rip
Hamilton and the total team defense on Michael Redd. He was-
n't a big factor in most of the games. When Tayshaun shined was

the series against Indiana. A lot of times Tayshaun is making it difficult for guys like Kobe to get off shots. He made the greatest block of all time against Indiana, and that's when I knew they were going to the Finals. When he made that block on Reggie Miller, I knew they weren't going to quit no matter what they faced. Rip was the knight in shining armor against Milwaukee."

But next loomed the New Jersey Nets, the two-time Eastern Conference champs, who had swept the Pistons the previous season and still had their three-headed monster of Jason Kidd, Richard Jefferson, and Kenyon Martin.

Finally Getting Past the Nets

"The Jersey series was more of a psychological series," said Mahorn. "New Jersey beat us last year and I think sometimes we looked past Milwaukee instead of taking care of business. That's why that series lasted as long as it did. It was 'Hey, we're going to beat Jersey, but we're going to beat them psychologically.' That was all psychological. They played above whatever circumstance presented itself and won the game. That was the key game of that series."

The Pistons held serve in the first two games at the Palace, pounding the Nets 78-56 in Game 1 with Prince and Hamilton scoring 15 points each and the hapless Nets scoring a franchise playoff low for points, shooting just 27.1 percent from the field. It was also the fewest points the Pistons allowed in a playoff game. The Nets rebounded to score 80 points in Game 2, but still lost by 15. Detroit's backcourt of Hamilton and Billups scored 28 points each and totally dominated Jason Kidd and Kerry Kittles, who combined for just 14 points.

New York's media machine was in hyperdrive, and it came up with a variety of reasons why the Nets were down 2-0 to the Pistons headed into Game 3, none of which was the fact that the Pistons just played two better games at home than their opponent.

"All we did is hold serve," said coach Larry Brown after the team's morning shootaround at John Jay College. "They say a series doesn't really start until a team wins on the opponent's home floor. Let's hope that's the case."

In the meantime, one of the theories was that Brown was out-coaching 33-year-old Lawrence Frank, completing his first season as a head coach after taking over for Byron Scott during the season.

"I don't buy that; I never buy into that stuff," said Brown. "When you make shots everybody looks good. I prepare them like I would for any game. I'm not making adjustments on the fly. I respect them over there. I don't buy that at all. Did they say he out-coached Lenny Wilkens? I don't buy that. I think this kid is really prepared. I look at the films and they've changed up. They've done a lot of new things that we haven't seen before. I watched them in the Knicks series. Every time they'd come out of a timeout they'd come out real serious. So I don't buy that at all. Players win games. Our job is to make sure we put our teams in a position to win games, and I think he has done that. That's what I've tried to do."

Theory 2: Jason Kidd couldn't be healthy if Billups was outplaying him.

Kidd missed most of the last two weeks of the season with a bone bruise in his knee. He averaged 8.5 points, 8.5 assists and seven rebounds in the two games in Detroit. Conversely, Billups averaged 17 points per game, including 28 in Game 2, 7.5 assists and three rebounds per game. Kidd shot just 26.9 percent from the field as the Pistons' defense made an effort to keep him out of the lane and shooting jumpers.

"Hey, we all have bumps and bruises this time of the season," said Lindsey Hunter. "I knew he was hurt in the latter part of the season. It's unfortunate for him, but we had to do what we have to do."

Kidd went out of his way after Saturday's practice to tell the media that he was fine.

"I looked forward to this series because I get a chance to play against Jason, who is considered the best point guard in the league," said Billups. "I had to step up and take that challenge. Maybe he's banged up, maybe he isn't. Everybody's banged up this time of the season. The ultimate competitors always play through it, and he's doing that."

The Nets Hold Serve

As well as the Pistons played in Games 1 and 2, they were equally as inept in Games 3 and 4 at East Rutherford.

Jefferson set a playoff scoring high with 30 points, and the Nets held the Pistons to 28.9 percent shooting from the field and 13 points in the first quarter in taking Game 3, 82-64.

It was a particularly difficult game for Ben Wallace, who was magnificent with 24 points and 15 rebounds in a losing cause. The game was played on Mother's Day, and Ben's mind was on his mother, Sadie, whom he buried a year before on the eve of his first All-Star appearance in Atlanta.

"It was just hard to be out there knowing it was Mother's Day," said Wallace. "I had her on my mind."

Game 4 didn't go much better for the Pistons on May 11 as the Nets held the Pistons to 79 points and won by 15. Hamilton was the only Piston in double figures with 30, while five Nets had at least 11 points, with Kidd's triple-double leading the way—22, points, 10 rebounds and 11 assists.

A War of Attrition

The Pistons returned home for Game 5 hoping to regain some of the momentum they lost at Continental Airlines Arena.

It turned out to be an epic battle that took three overtimes to settle because Billups banked in a 43-footer at the buzzer to send the game into overtime tied at 88.

A total of eight players fouled out, four on each side, and Brian Scalabrine, a curly redhead from Southern California, proved to be the hero. He scored 17 points off the bench, made six of seven field goal attempts and all four of his three-point attempts in helping the Nets to a 127-120 victory, giving New Jersey a 3-2 edge in the series, heading to Detroit for what could have been a clinching Game 6.

Rip Comes up Big

Having played two bad games in Jersey, there was no reason to think the Pistons could turn it around with their season on the line, but they did.

There are no more questions about why Joe Dumars traded Jerry Stackhouse for Richard Hamilton. There's no more head scratching or wondering about would Hamilton be strong enough or experienced enough to answer the challenge of being the No. 1 scorer on a team that was going places. He has answered all the questions and won over one of the toughest critics he'll ever play for: Brown.

Hamilton's 18-foot jumper with 15.5 seconds left proved to be the winning shot in the Pistons' 81-75 victory in their elimination game at New Jersey, forcing the series to ship back to the Palace for Game 7.

Other than Ben Wallace, Hamilton, despite his lean 6'7", 193-pound build, might be the toughest Piston. He gets banged around, knocked around, pushed, shoved and belted, but he keeps getting up.

"This kid, every single day, comes to practice and tries to get better, and he's not afraid of taking a big shot," said Brown. "I think when they were making a rally, the only guy who was looking to score was him. It wasn't his fault. I don't think we gave him much help, but his improvement has been amazing."

This comes from a coach who rides Mike James at every turn and is emphatic about players playing the right way to the point of risking Mehmet Okur, a restricted free agent who's starving for playing time."

The previous season was Hamilton's first trip into the playoffs and he passed the test, starting all 17 games and averaged 22.5 points per game while shooting 44.2 percent from the field and 90.6 from the free throw line. The next postseason, he was even better. His scoring was down, but his overall play was better; his assists and rebounds are both up.

"He has one of the best mid-range games in the league," admitted Kidd after Hamilton's pump fake got him up in the air and gave him enough room for the game-clinching field goal.

"He's their main scorer and we knew they were going to look for him. He made a tough shot. At first I thought he was just trying to draw the foul, but he made a tough shot."

Hamilton thought he got fouled on the play, but stayed with the shot before yelping at the refs after he made the field goal.

After the Nets got off to a quick 13-2 lead, it was Hamilton who sparked the team's 48-23 run that gave them a 50-36 halftime lead.

"When Kidd was on me I just tried to make him work," said Hamilton. "I thought I could shoot over him if I could get to a certain spot on the floor. That's what I was trying to do, get to a spot and get the shot over him."

The reason Hamilton had drawn praise from Brown is that his game has evolved from more than just being a scorer. Dumars openly challenged Hamilton to be more than a guy who could average 20 points per game. He told him he was cheating himself if he thought that's all he could do to help the team. That's when Hamilton's defense got better and his assists went up.

He averaged 10 assists his last three regular season games and had 11 assists before fouling out of Friday's triple overtime loss at the Palace.

"I believe I can run out there all day, so I never worry about fatigue," said Hamilton.

"We have guys on this team who can score. We're a very confident group. Somebody asked before the game why did we look so loose? That's because we knew what we had to do.

Richard Hamilton (left) was a big reason that the Pistons finally got past the Nets. (AP/WWP)

"You live for situations like this. When you're in the back yard playing and you're counting down the final seconds, you dream about hitting a shot over a Jason Kidd, a guy I've been watching my whole career."

Said Chauncey Billups: "Rip had some fresh legs because he didn't play that much the other day. He was like the computer game when you hit the speed button. He was playing faster than anybody else. He hit some huge shots and made some great defensive plays, and those are the things we expect out of him. I think he's the best player in the game coming off screens. He's 6'7", so once he gets it up it's tough to block it and it's tough to make him change. Jason is a good defender and he has done a good job, but Rip was a tough cover for anybody."

Near the end of the Nets' regular season, Kidd was sidelined with a bone bruise in his knee. Kenyon Martin also was sidelined with tendonitis. That left Richard Jefferson to be the go-to guy, chief scoring threat and leader of the team while two of the Big Three sat.

While Larry Brown tried to devise ways to stop him for Game 7, he knew he would get a chance to coach him this summer at the Summer Olympic Games in Athens, Greece. That's when Brown would really appreciate the development of Jefferson, a third-year forward from Arizona who has elevated himself to near All-Star status. For the playoffs Jefferson averaged 20.1 points per game and shot 41.8 percent from the field. Against the Pistons, he averaged 21.7 going into Game 7.

"I think when Jason and Kenyon got hurt it really helped them prepare for now," said Brown. "They really focused on getting Richard the ball, and he delivered. I think that was the real plus out of those injuries. I look at this series and the kid's been phenomenal. I watched them against the Knicks and at the end of the season. He's on the Olympic team."

With Jefferson's rise to stardom, Prince, the small forward assigned to guard him, took his lumps. Brown never once thought about taking Prince out of the starting lineup; everyone in the organization knew that he was the only small forward in the organization capable of keeping up with Jefferson at both ends of the floor.

"Have I been frustrated? Not at all," said Prince. "The way I've been playing in this series: to force a Game 7 and have it 3-3. Pretty much in this playoff series the way I've been playing has determined how we've been winning games. For us to get to a Game 7 the way I've been shooting the basketball is unbelievable. For me to be worried at all after the way we won Game 6, there's nothing for me to be worried about."

After a great series against Milwaukee and Desmond Mason, Prince shot just 30.5 percent from the field and averaged just eight points and five rebounds per game.

Prince admitted that Rasheed Wallace or Mehmet Okur at the three spot causes more problems for the Nets than the team's smaller lineup when the reserves come in.

"For the most part Jefferson had the most minutes on the floor, and they've been running pick-and-roll with Kidd to see how we play that," said Prince. "They try to run a post up or isolation that way. I just think the reason why he has played well all year long is the reason why they had trust to run plays for him at the end of the game. That comes with the way he has been playing all year and what he has been doing in this series. Martin has been in foul trouble and Kidd hasn't shot the ball that well the whole series. That's why they've been going to him."

Closing Out the Series

Sparked by the win in Game 6, the Pistons totally domi-nated Game 7, hammering the Nets into submission with a 90-69 triumph that propelled them to the conference finals for the second straight year.

Four Pistons scored in double figures with Hamilton and Billups combining for 43 points while the defense held the Nets to 35.8 percent shooting with Kidd going scoreless for the first time in a playoff game. The Nets were running on empty while the Pistons were running to Indianapolis to face the team with the best record in the NBA.

Chapter 11

THE 2004 PLAYOFFS

Best of the East

With Wallace in tow, the Pistons traveled to Indiana's Conseco Fieldhouse on May 22, with the winner of the best-of-seven series advancing to the NBA Finals.

The last time the two met during the regular season, the Pistons hung a 79-61 thumping on the Pacers, but this time, the stakes were a little bit higher.

The Stories Within the Series

"There were a lot of subplots in the Indiana series," said Mahorn. "You had a coach who coached this team to Eastern Conference finals the year before and you had Larry Brown coming in and taking over. I don't think Rick Carlisle exploited the weaknesses of the Pistons. Things you should know from being with the team the previous year, he didn't really take advantage of. Rasheed not being there was a difference, but besides him there were the same people. You should know what your players' weaknesses and strengths are. He did a good job and the scores weren't that high. Rick had to deal with the low post play. He didn't have the guards to handle Detroit. He made the right adjustments, but a lot of times it comes with the territory to put the right guys in and how the guys are going to play.

"You have to protect home court to win a championship. The Piston fans in Game 5 at Indiana were unbelievable. The place was ringing 'Let's go Pistons' and people were walking around there like the game was at the Palace. Emotionally that pumps you up when you're louder than the crowd that is there for the home team. The home crowd didn't give them what they needed in that game. You're playing on the road and you thought it was our house when you got your fans there. That's a beautiful blessing. You play even harder.

"When you heard 'Deeetroit Basketball' coming from the fans you were ready to ball. Chauncey Billups showed what he could do in that series and I really think that's when he distinguished himself."

"In playing Indiana, the only difference is we had to play the first two games on the road, but we're a good road team," said Billups. "That's a team that beat us three out of four times, so we're looking for some payback. It should be a very good series, too."

Mehmet Okur hoped to show his old coach, Rick Carlisle, what he could do, especially if Coach Brown employed his big-man lineup of Ben and Rasheed Wallace along with Okur. He didn't.

"I think against New Jersey it really threw them off seeing so many big guys out there," said Okur. "Maybe we can try this against Indiana. I am ready for Indiana."

Brown's Old Team, Sort Of

Larry Brown coached Indiana for four seasons, but Reggie Miller was the only player left on the Pacers' roster from when Larry Brown coached there in the 1990s. Miller delivered the first blow in the series, nailing a three with 31.7 seconds left to break a 74-all tie and send the Pacers to a 78-74 victory in Game 1. Miller scored the last four points for the Pacers to seal the game after being badly outplayed by Richard Hamilton, who scored 23 to lead all scorers. It was Miller's only field goal of the game.

"It was the kind of game everybody expected, intense and not really high scoring," said Carlisle. "When they went up by two on the Prince shot, it was gut-check time. Jeff Foster made a big play when the play had broken down, and [Jamaal] Tinsley got the ball and made a simple call and he was ready to make a call to Reggie, who was due to do something because he was having a tough night. Jeff was also the guy who made the screen on Reggie's three, so he was big. We had a lot of guys step forward.

"The thing about Reggie, as games get tighter, he's the kind of guy that focuses in even more. It was certainly time, because we were having troubles."

Back and Forth in the Fourth

Down three to start the fourth, Hamilton scored the first four points of the period on a jumper and layup, forcing the Pacers to call a timeout facing a one-point deficit, 62-61. Ron

Artest missed a jumper and Mike James found Ben for a lob dunk to put the Pistons ahead 64-61.

Tinsley led the comeback with a runner in the lane and to put the Pacers up 70-68 with 6:51 left to play and Ben on the bench with a sore lip courtesy of taking a shot from O'Neal's head.

Jeff Foster tied it up on a layup, and when Billups missed a three, the Pacers took a 77-74 lead on a three from Miller with 31.7 left.

Hamilton missed his own three and Ben fouled O'Neal on the rebound with 19.8 left. O'Neal missed both with Prince grabbing the rebound and calling a timeout.

Billups and Rasheed missed triples that could've tied the game, but it wasn't to be for the visitors.

The Guarantee

After Game 1, Rasheed Wallace, who scored just four points and missed six of seven shots from the field, guaranteed a victory in Game 2. Rasheed declared: "I'm guaranteeing Game 2. That's the bottom line. That's all I'm saying. They will not win Game 2, you heard that from me. Y'all can print whatever you want. Put it on the front page, back page, middle of the page. They will not win Game 2."

Surely, a day later Rasheed would backtrack a little from his bold boast that Game 2 would be a victory, especially after hanging out with former Portland teammate and Indiana star Jermaine O'Neal during the evening?

Nope.

That's not Wallace's style, but Joe Dumars, the team's president of basketball operations, knew that when he traded for

Rasheed on February 19. He realized there would be days like this, so even if he might have cringed on the inside, he would leave it up to Rasheed to go out and help back up his prediction.

"I said it last night and I'm saying it again, we will win Game 2," said Rasheed. "I'm not trying to sound ignorant or anything, but we will win."

Backing up Rasheed's Words

Rasheed's teammates were not angered at all by the bold prediction.

"I got his back, baby," said Billups. "I'm not mad at him at all. I think that's just the confidence he has in us as a team and that we squandered one away. You have to have confidence in your teammates to say that against a team that has won more games than anybody this year and you're playing them on their court. That's just confidence, and also we feel like we lost the game; we beat ourselves and they didn't beat us. We feel like if we play the same way and are given the same opportunity, we can win it."

"Ain't no pressure on me," said Ben Wallace when asked about Rasheed's bold prediction after his terrific performance in Game 1 with 22 rebounds, 11 points, five blocked shots and five assists in 39 minutes. "We put pressure on ourselves. We're ready. We have to prepare ourselves. If that's what it takes, then that's what it takes. We put ourselves in a tough situation. We just have to come out and play basketball."

Confidence or locker room fodder, Rasheed clearly placed the spotlight on himself and deflected some of the glare from his teammates.

"I think it was in the heat of the moment," said Brown. "He was upset with the way the game went, and he just said that. But we have to play. It ain't about Rasheed only, it's about all of us. We've got to get it done."

"It was our offense that lost us the game," said Billups. "We played good. We expect that kind of effort every night. We didn't execute on offense, but we'll take that kind of effort on defense. I thought Tayshaun [Prince] did a great job of defending [Ron] Artest and Rasheed did a great job of using his length to bother Jermaine O'Neal."

Maybe that's why Rasheed made his prediction. After all, the Pistons held the Pacers to 33 percent shooting from the field. Artest and O'Neal combined to go just 13 of 43 from the field. Miller, who hit the game-winning shot with 31.7 seconds left, had just one field goal.

"We turned the ball over and took bad shots," said Brown. "We've got to get to the free throw line. Jermaine played the whole game with one foul. Artest played the whole game with just one foul. Our whole team was in foul trouble the first half; then Rasheed and Ben were in foul trouble, so it impacts how you played. If their big guys aren't going to get fouls and ours do, we can't nearly be as aggressive offensively."

Tying the Series

It was Guaran-Sheed, and Rasheed Wallace had his teammates to thank for fulfilling his Game 2 prophecy.

The key play? Detroit's 19th block of the game, a team playoff record. Prince, running in a full sprint from halfcourt, ran down Reggie Miller, who was swooping in for an uncontested layup after a Piston turnover, and knocked the ball away before diving into a crowd of Pacer fans.

"I'm sure Reggie Miller thought he had an easy one; I was just hoping he'd get to the ball before its down-flight," said Ben Wallace, who sat out most of the first half in foul trouble. "People said Tayshaun had been struggling at the offensive end, but defensively he's been there all year for us."

Said Brown: "It was one of the greatest hustle plays I've ever seen, and Rip [Hamilton] was equally as alert in tracking the ball down. We got completely lost at the end because of the things happening out there."

Dumars just shook his head when asked if that was one of the most specutacular blocks he had seen.

"With what was at stake and the way it happened, definitely," he said. "It was incredible."

Prince was not the only member of the block party. Rasheed had five blocked shots and Ben and Prince four each.

"It was a heck of a play," said Jermaine O'Neal, who was just six of 18 from the field. "He almost killed himself, but those are the types of plays you have to make, and I'm sure you'll see a lot more."

Back to Auburn Hills

Detroit returned home and beat the Pacers 85-78 in Game 3 as Rasheed and Hamilton both scored 20 to offset the 24 points by O'Neal. The Pistons survived a playoff-low nine

This Tayshaun Prince block that preserved Detroit's Game 2 victory may have been the key play of the series and the entire postseason. (AP/WWP)

points in the second quarter to squeak out the victory while holding the Pacers to 34.7 percent shooting.

Keeping home court with a Game 4 victory would have made the Pistons' life a lot easier, but Detroit was never a team that did things the easy way throughout the season. The Pistons shot just 30.8 percent in Game 4 and scored just 68 points in an 83-68 loss. Hamilton and Billups combined for 43 points, but their teammates could muster just 25. Carlisle started Austin Croshere in place of Jeff Foster, and the reserve forward scored 14 points to keep the home team off balance. Carlisle said afterward that the Pistons' season would be broken if they didn't advance to the NBA Finals because they were supposed to get there after what happened the year before.

Breaking the 2-2 Tie

Game 5 on May 30 was memorable for the Pistons in Indianapolis because it had a strange feel throughout the day.

It started with a tornado that ending up touching down about four miles from Conseco Fieldhouse, to the Indianapolis 500 being hindered by the weather, to more Pistons than Pacers fans being in the arena when the doors opened at 5:30 p.m. Central Time, donning wigs, signs and throwback jerseys.

It culminated in Richard Hamilton torching the Pacers' Ron Artest and Reggie Miller in a crucial Game 5 with all 30 of his 33 points through three quarters in the Pistons 83-65 victory.

"We just wanted to come out and hit first," said Hamilton. "We wanted to come out and not get down and get on top early. I think it was all mental from the last game. We had an opportunity to make some ground up last game and we came out relaxed and we ended up playing a way that we're not used to. We said we'd play together at both ends of the floor. Move the ball side to side and make plays. Both teams are great defensive teams and do a great job of zoning up. When I was in Washington, Coach Doug Collins said if you keep moving nobody can guard that."

Detroit held another block party at Conseco, rejecting 13 shots by the home team for 32 in their last two road games in Indiana.

"I've never been on the road and had that much fan support before," said Corliss Williamson, who had five points off the bench. "At times it sounded like a home game. When we came out to warm up early they were everywhere. It makes you feel good when you get that kind of support. Those are true Pistons fans, not the ones that were booing us during Game 4."

"We didn't bring the same energy we had in Detroit," said Miller, who scored just five points. "Most of our principles went out the window tonight. He [Hamilton] did a great job of moving, especially off the screens. Sometimes we'd send one or two defenders at him. By the fourth quarter he had already been on a roll."

Striking the Final Blow

More players watch the NBA Finals than participate in it, so a day before the biggest game of their careers, the Pistons and coach Larry Brown talked about what was at stake when the Pistons got a chance to close out the series with a victory at home against the Pacers.

*Richard Hamilton was able to successfully score against the Pacers'
defensive stopper, Ron Artest. (AP/WWP)*

"We talked about it," said Brown. "When we started this playoffs, guys like Elden [Campbell] and Rasheed [Wallace] and my brother [Herb] and me and Woody [Mike Woodson]; guys who have been in it a long time kind of expressed how few opportunities you have. You have to make the most of it because it doesn't happen to every team. This team went to the conference finals last year and got beat four straight. I told them you don't always get back to the finals, so to have an opportunity to go to the NBA Finals is an incredible achievement."

You would think that with a big victory in Game 5, the momentum would be in the Pistons' favor heading into Game 6, but backup center Elden Campbell said beware.

"With the games switching the way they have there's no momentum," said Campbell. "Each game is a separate, isolated incident. We have to remember what we did well and learn from our mistakes."

Blood and Guts

His nose bloodied by a blow from Defensive Player of the Year Artest, Hamilton delivered the knockout punch that sent Indy, the best team record-wise in the NBA, home for the summer and the Pistons to their first NBA Finals since 1990.

Hamilton scored nine of his 21 points in the fourth and the Pistons prevailed 69-65 at the Palace to win the best-of-seven series 4-2. A sellout crowd of 22,076, which included Chuck Daly, Bill Laimbeer, Mahorn, and Dumars, had to sit on the edge of their seats as Indy led for most of the game.

Detroit led for just three minutes, 57 seconds of the game, but they were the final 3:57. Hamilton led four Pistons in double figures as Ben Wallace had 12 points and 16 rebounds, Rasheed Wallace 11 points and 11 rebounds and Chauncey Billups 10.

As he walked in the locker room Rasheed said, "This silver trophy is nice, but I like the gold one better."

He was referring to the Larry O'Brien trophy that goes to the NBA champs.

By virtue of losing two games at home, the banged-up Pacers sealed their own fate despite a valiant effort in Game 6.

Jermaine O'Neal had 20 for the Pacers and Artest 11. Indy shot just 36.4 percent from the field and 32 points in the second half.

"It's crazy, it still hasn't sunk in yet," said Hamilton, who came to the game in a Magic Johnson Lakers jersey. "It's unbelievable because you know where I come from and now being able to play for a world title is crazy. It starts with those guys in the locker room, especially Coach [Larry] Brown. He has done an excellent job from day one."

O'Neal and Rasheed were teammates at Portland, and they hugged afterward.

"I told him good luck and I hope they represent the Eastern Conference well," said O'Neal.

Joe's Ulcer

"This can't be good for you," said Dumars, rubbing his hand on his stomach. "As a player you can make a shot or make a pass, but sitting up there watching....I tell my wife [Debbie] all the time that this can't be good for you. It's definitely different from being a player.

"From day one of training camp and the dinner we had just before the playoffs started, I told these guys I wanted nothing less than going to the Finals."

Artest's Hit

Artest was hit with a flagrant foul when he hit Hamilton with a forearm to the face, causing his nose to bleed with 3:57 left.

He made both to make it 61-59, and possession stayed with the Pistons as Artest argued he was hit first. Rasheed dunked in a Billups miss while Hamilton was being called for a technical foul with 3:44 left. Miller missed the free throw as Indy still trailed by four.

"I thought it was a cheap shot," said Hamilton. "But I just kept on playing. That's part of basketball. I'm happy I got hit because sometimes it takes getting hit like that to get you right, ready and focused. We knew if it was a close game our chances were great."

Said Lindsey Hunter, who made his second trip to the NBA Finals: "I was just hoping that Rip wouldn't lose his cool and retaliate, which he eventually did. It was a big play. We never make things easy on ourselves. We seem to always do things the hard way."

Added Ben Wallace: "I thought the flagrant foul was a black eye to this game. This isn't an individual game and you have to be aware of the other four guys on the floor. It was unfortunate. It hurts your team."

Chapter 12

THE FINALS

With 81 playoff victories, Brown had the most of any coach who hadn't won an NBA title. Three years ago the Lakers beat his Philadelphia 76ers. With his first Pistons squad, he got his second chance at a ring against Kobe and Shaq, and with a team that believed he could get them there.

The series was hailed as the Lakers' Fab Four of Shaq, Kobe, Karl Malone, and Gary Payton against the underdog Pistons.

Rick Mahorn on the Lakers' and Pistons' Game Plans

"The Lakers relied on the five guys they had on the court," said Mahorn. "They wanted Kobe and Shaq to carry the load. You knew Shaq was going to get his if he got the ball. When we started Game 1 in Los Angeles the guys were focued in on what they were going to do. They didn't have any scoring punch off the bench. All you had to do was play against the starting five. L.A. missed Robert Horry and Brian Shaw, guys who could make the outside shot. You figured Kobe was going to shoot the ball like he did and not let Shaq get involved. I would have kept giving the ball to Shaq. There was more pressure on us to win at home than it was for the Lakers to split on the road. In '88 we spilt at home and that was the problem. In this series we came home and won all three games, which had never been done before. It would've been tough to go back to L.A. That was the difference. That overtime game was a gimme. The guys knew they gave one away and they knew they had to come home and make up for it. I thought Body [Ben Wallace] was huge once the team got home. Once he gets it in his mind what he wants to do, he goes out and does it. I know he outplayed Shaq, but you have to figure Shaq is a different meaning for L.A., and Body is a different meaning for Detroit. He took it on his shoulders and played the kind of game you knew would come out and play. Each guy on the Pistons had a role, and Ben relished his role. The 22 rebounds and 18 points; that's all you need to know."

Winning One for Coach Brown

"He [Larry Brown] has been successful everywhere he has been," said Ben Wallace. "He just doesn't assume you know how to play the game. When he first got here we didn't really know what to expect, but once he got here we understand why he has succeeded everywhere he had been. He gets out and teaches the fundamentals of the game, and I think that's a lost art in this league."

From what the players say, Brown isn't a dictator. He allowed players to be part of game plans, and during games he asks for advice to accomplish what he's trying to get done out on the floor.

"I love playing for Coach Brown," said Richard Hamilton. "I think he has made me a better player. Obviously, we're a better team."

Getting Off to a Great Start

Shaq did his thing. Kobe did his thing and the two superstars combined for 59 points. However it was the Pistons, with leading scoring Richard Hamilton laboring through a poor shooting night and contributing just 12 points, coming through and ripping home court away from the heavily favored Lakers in an upset.

Leading throughout the second half and getting solid performances from just about everybody that played, the Pistons' defense shut down the rest of the Lakers and hammered out a 87-75 win in Game 1.

Two of the Lakers' big four delivered. Shaquille O'Neal scored 34 and Kobe Bryant had 25, but the rest of the Laker starters combined for just 12 points with Karl Malone scoring just four on two of nine shooting and Gary Payton three on one of four shooting.

"Tayshaun [Prince] did a good job on Kobe," said Rasheed Wallace. "He got by him for a couple of jumpers, but you just have to stay with it. We're excited, but it's a race to four. We can't get overzealous over one win. That's how teams come out and lose the next game. We just have to stay focused."

Rasheed Wallace and all his teammates played well, and the Pistons stunned the Lakers in Game 1 of the 2004 NBA Finals. (AP/WWP)

Stepping up for the Pistons

Richard Hamilton made just five of 16 shots with six turnovers, five assists and seven rebounds, so Chauncey Billups filled the void, leading the Pistons with 22 and four assists, Rasheed Wallace fought through foul trouble with 14 and Tayshaun Prince had 11 and a bundle of good defensive plays with four assists and six rebounds and two steals.

"I wanted to come out and be aggressive," said Billups. "We wanted to come out and get them involved as much as possible in the pick-and-roll. I'm a shooter. I can score the ball. If you're setting the pick and nobody's there I'm going to shoot it. When you have myself or Rip handling the ball and Rasheed or Ben or Mehmet Okur setting the pick, you pick your poison."

Ben Wallace had eight rebounds and nine points in his battle with Shaq.

"We as a team didn't come out with much energy," said O'Neal. "I don't think a person going 13 of 16 means he's tired. This puts a lot of pressure on us for the next game. Detroit comes out and plays great defense and they're aggressive.

"They wanted it a little more than we did. We were lackluster. We just have to play better overall as a team. We didn't shoot the ball well tonight. It felt pretty good not getting doubled. I could do what I wanted to do.

"Tayshaun did a great job of staying with Kobe and contesting his shot. And Tayshaun's the kind of player who can hit shots and he did that."

Adjustments Heading into Game 2

"We don't know what they are going to do, but I think we're able to adjust to whatever type of defense they throw," said Shaquille O'Neal. "You know, we've had many defenses thrown at us over the past nine months, over the past couple of years, so we should be able to adjust to anything.

"I think it has gotten our attention. We realize that this team is not going to lay down because the Lakers are in the building. We really have to go out and play. It's not anything they did to throw us out of our game. I just think it's more us. We've just got to keep everybody involved and we've just got to want it."

Whether it's Shaq's 7'1", 360-pound-plus frame or the fact that his team was up 1-0 in the series, Brown was in no mood to argue.

"If he says so," Brown said of O'Neal's comments before laughter broke out in the interview room at the Staples Center.

"I mean, I've watched them play. I don't think it was a typical Laker game. You know, I don't know how many times in Payton's career or Karl Malone's career they are going to have a game like that, where they weren't involved a lot. And I don't know how many times they are going to score 75 points at home in a playoff home game.

"But I thought we played pretty good, personally. We shot 47 percent, we rebounded the ball effectively, we had four turnovers in the second half. We had a lot of contributions from a lot of people, so you know in my eyes, we played pretty darn good. I won't dispute Shaq's assessment of the way they played. That's not a typical Laker game."

However, the Pistons believed that losing home court against the Milwaukee Bucks in Round 1, losing a triple overtime game at home to New Jersey and having to win the last two games of that series to advance and winning two games at Indiana, where no team had won in the playoffs to that point, prepared them for Shaq and the mighty Lakers.

They expected Shaq to shoot the ball more, Kobe to shoot less, and the rest of the Lakers to make more of a contribution.

Game 2: The Shot

It's a question that could have haunted Brown and the Pistons for years to come if they had lost the championship series. Should they have fouled Kobe Bryant with a three-point lead and the ball in Bryant's hands late in regulation of Game 2?

They didn't, Bryant scored, the game went into overtime and the Lakers got back in the series with a 99-91 victory.

"We don't foul in a situation like that," said Brown. "He's so athletic that he's going to go up with that shot. I just thought about a four-point play. We switched and wanted to get a hand up. We talked about switching everything because they needed a three. We switched off and kind of backed off.

"I thought Shaq's offensive rebound and three-point play was the big play the possession before that. Kobe made a great shot. We didn't handle the clock great and took half-assed shots. They made a huge play and it got into overtime and we lost our poise. We're crushed."

Game 3: Rasheed Steps Up

Rasheed Wallace had his teammates' and coaches' permission to be a little greedy.

After Game 2, Brown was particularly perturbed at the lack of respect his 6'11" center/forward got from the referees.

"He gets the ball two feet from the basket, and by the time he goes to take a shot, he's 12 feet away," said Brown. "I think he has handled the situation quite well considering what's happening to him. He's emotional, but the thing that bothers me is they'll call something at one end, then when the same thing happens to Rasheed, he doesn't understand why he doesn't get the same call. I don't understand it either, but we need him out there."

In both games in L.A., Rasheed spent a lot of the first half watching from the bench because of foul problems.

"He had it going in the third quarter, and when he has it going it forces them to double-team," said Hamilton. "It gets us wide-open looks on the perimeter. We need to get him the ball not just at the beginning of the game, but throughout the game."

"He has been great," said Hamilton. "He does so many great things for the team, especially defensively. He might be too unselfish. I just know we need to give him the ball more."

Game 4: Shaq and Not Much Else

L.A. fed the Diesel, argued with the referees, committed 33 fouls and still lost, 88-80.

O'Neal dominated the paint with 36 points on 16 of 21 shooting from the field, and 20 rebounds, but Rasheed Wallace, after a night of bowling with his friends and his kids, had his best scoring game of the series with 26 points, 10 coming in the crucial minutes of the fourth quarter. Rasheed made 10 of 23 field goal attempts and had 13 rebounds and made all six of his free throw attempts.

"Hell yeah it's a misperception that I can't go down low," said Rasheed. "I've always been in the post and I didn't start going outside until I started playing the three [small forward] at Portland. I've had some big games. I just have to keep working. It felt good for the first time in this series to play in the second quarter. I still have a foul or two, but I just had to play through it and keep that determination. My shots were falling and it was my night."

His night came at the right time. "Somebody said he was going to get 20 tonight," said Brown. "He was great on both ends. We got a little out of sync at times offensively. Again, we had five assists in the first half. He got great looks. In the second half Chauncey [Billups] and Rip [Hamilton] and Tayshaun [Prince] started coming off screens and looking for him.

"I told them how proud I was of them. No matter how you look at it, you have to win four games in a series, and that's what we talked about."

A Wasted Effort from Shaq

"I'm very upset," said O'Neal. "We had it, but we made some mistakes in the fourth quarter. We know we can play with this team, but we haven't shown it yet. It comes down to Game 5 and we have to give it what we have. It was a sloppy fourth quarter for us. The pressure is on them to close us out."

Shaq became the first player since Bob Pettit on March 24, 1963, to record a 30-point, 20-rebound game against the Pistons in the playoffs.

O'Neal kept scoring inside, but the Pistons were getting offense from Hamilton, Billups and Rasheed while Bryant continued to fire blanks.

Staying on Focus

"I wasn't thinking about winning the championship after Game 4," said Rasheed Wallace, whose 26 points and 13 rebounds were crucial in the Game 4 victory. "I just want to get one more win. I'm not thinking about how I'm going to celebrate or what this all means. I'm just preparing to go out and play as hard as I can. This would be good for Pound-for-Pound [Larry Brown] and the team, but we're not there yet. We haven't done anything yet, because like I said before the series goes to four. Everybody's going to go home and do what they usually do: relax, eat, spend time with family."

Dumars, twice a champion and MVP of the 1989 Finals, pulled up to the Palace and spotted a local reporter. He rolled down his window and didn't say a word. He just stuck one finger in the air, meaning one more victory and he could rest some demons that have hounded him all year as far as firing Carlisle for Brown and drafting Milicic instead of Carmelo Anthony.

With a 3-1 lead in the series, the Pistons were one game away from the organization's third NBA title, but as Kobe Bryant pointed out, history wasn't on either team's side.

No team had ever won three straight home games in the 2-3-2 Finals format. When the Pistons won Game 5, they became the first to accomplish that goal.

Geting to this stage for Brown made him appreciate Jackson and his nine championships as a coach even more.

"No matter how you look at it, one team is standing at the end," said Brown. "And being here now, I'm amazed at what Phil's accomplished. It's just so hard to get here, but I probably would be smarter if it happened."

R-E-S-P-E-C-T

In each of the Pistons' first two championships, the team closed out the finals on the road. So for title number three, it was a nice change to give the hometown fans a chance to witness history and the team's third championship in one of the great upsets considering few gave Detroit a chance to win the game, let alone the series.

Detroit became the first home team ever to win three straight home games to clinch a championship, doing it in obliterating fashion with one of their best overall performances of the season, beating Los Angeles to every rebound, every loose ball and shooting at a 50 percent clip throughout most of the game to bomb the Lakers, 100-87.

Ben Wallace, playing at warp speed while everyone else appeared on slow play, dominated the action at both ends with 22 rebounds and 18 points and buckets full of energy.

Tayshaun Prince was brilliant at both ends with his own double-double, 17 points and 10 rebounds, and was exhausted as he left the floor with one minute, 59 seconds left.

Richard Hamilton finally got an upper hand on high school rival Kobe Bryant, who was hounded into his worst Finals performance ever by Prince. Hamilton finished with 21 points and four assists. He held his mask in the air, the one that has protected his surgically repaired nose, as he left the court.

Meanwhile, the Lakers' Fantastic Four looked like the Fumbling Four as they lost their cool, took bad shots and didn't get the ball inside to a tired Shaquille O'Neal enough after he played 47 minutes of Game 4.

The loss ended the run for Jackson, Kobe and Shaq. Jackson's contract wasn't renewed. Shaq was traded to Miami for Lamar Odom, Brian Grant and Caron Butler. Meanwhile, Kobe reportedly signed the richest contract in NBA history at $136 million-plus.

Deconstructing the Big Upset

"Teams beat individuals, and we picked the wrong time to be individuals," said Laker forward Rick Fox, who put it better than anybody.

The fractured Lakers were no match for the team Dumars and Brown put together this season, culminating in one of the biggest upsets in NBA Finals history.

"Nobody gave us a chance, but we didn't read the papers or listen to the TV guys or listen to all the talk," said Lindsey Hunter, who tied childhood idol Isiah Thomas for championship rings with two. "We just went out there and played hard and defended and shared the ball."

In fact, so many Pistons played well and made so may key contributions that there was no clear-cut most valuable player. Usually the Tim Duncans and Shaquille O'Neals and Michael Jordans dominate play so that their names are engraved on the trophy before the final horn sounds. Chauncey Billups won the award and deservedly so, but it easily could have been given to four of his teammates or a former Piston who wore No. 4 and now is the brains behind the organization.

"I think that's the uniqueness of this club," said Brown. "You can point to a lot of different individuals and feel pretty confident that that would have been a good choice. But when you look Chauncey's career, it's a lot like mine. I think I might have been a couple of more places than him, but he's still, you know, he has been through a lot."

MVP Candidate #1: Chauncey Billups

Here's a player almost half the league didn't want: Boston, Toronto, Orlando, Denver and Minnesota let him go at various times in his career. Dumars saw something in him that most didn't and signed him in 2002. He's now the point guard of point guards, leading the Pistons throughout the playoffs with big shots while looking for his teammates enough to keep Brown off his back. Billups scored 14 points in the clincher, but took just five shots, making three while making all eight of his free throw attempts and handing out six assists.

He dominated Gary Payton and he dominated Jason Kidd except for one game. The Lakers tried Kobe Bryant, Payton and Derek Fisher, but were never able to slow down the muscular guard.

"One thing I've learned from Coach Brown, and I feel equally satisfied with, is that I don't have to take a lot of shots in some games to be as effective, and that's one of the beautiful things that Coach has taught me," said Billups. "I've bought into that and I really believe now. So I knew today, even before

NBA ComissionerDavid Stern handed the MVP Trophy to Chauncey Billups, but a number of Pistons could have received the award. (AP/WWP)

the game started, I knew it wasn't going to be a day for me to shoot a whole lot of shots because I really wanted to control the tempo of the game."

Said Brown: "A lot of people told him he couldn't do certain things. Joe believed in him. And this is a shining moment for him, because he played against some pretty darned good players throughout the series. You look at the guys he had to play against. Jason Kidd and any number of great players, but this is the true beauty of a kid that's hung in there and maybe he's feeling like I do. You know, I got on him a lot. I challenged him a lot and I hope that he would feel that this is the reward of all of that. I certainly feel that way."

MVP Candidate #2: Ben Wallace

He was unbelievably spectacular in Game 5 with 22 rebounds and 18 points. Nobody in a Laker uniform could put a body on him or keep him off the boards. He was driving to the basket, blocking shots and dunking home misses by his teammates to will his team to a victory. He danced afterward, held his young son Bryce, and had the biggest smile of any of his teammates. He averaged 10 points and 14.3 rebounds for the playoffs and always set the tone with his defense and energy. The best help-side defender in the game, Wallace took offense to critics saying he wasn't a good one-on-one defender. Just ask the Lakers. They might be singing a different tune.

MVP Candidate #3: Tayshaun Prince

Ruben Patterson labeled himself the Kobe Stopper, but the job Prince did on Bryant throughout the series was better than any player who had ever taken on Bryant in the Finals.

Fouled hard by O'Neal early in the last game, Prince stepped up to the challenge, taking his lanky frame inside for 17 points and 10 tough rebounds. After the Milwaukee series his scoring suffered, but he took on some of the toughest scorers in the playoffs in Richard Jefferson, Ron Artest, Reggie Miller and Bryant.

"It doesn't get any better than Kobe," said Prince. "He was the greatest challenge. My teammates gave me a lot of support. We just tried to keep him from driving to the basket and tried to keep him out of the middle of the lane."

MVP Candidate #4: Richard Hamilton

His offense carried the Pistons through the first three rounds, and after two subpar games by Hamilton's standard, he broke free for 31 points in the Pistons' Game 3 victory at home. He wore out the likes of Reggie Miller, Artest, and even Kobe, with his nonstop movement on the offensive end and running his defender into screens set by Ben Wallace and Rasheed Wallace. For the playoffs, he averaged a team-high 21.5 points per game and chipped in 4.2 assists and 4.6 rebounds. He became a complete player and the Washington Wizards rue the day they traded him for Jerry Stackhouse.

"That was tough," said Hamilton. "It was like when you were young and you broke up with your girlfriend. Now, I

Richard Hamilton contributed on offense and defense throughout the 2004 playoffs. (AP/WWP)

wouldn't want to be anywhere else. I love these guys and we love each other. We sacrificed a lot for one common goal."

MVP Candidate #5: Rasheed Wallace

His biggest contribution wasn't the 26 points and 13 rebounds he had that gave the Pistons an insurmountable 3-1 lead in Game 4. It was the day the Pistons traded for him. He made the Pistons better, and to a man they say the crown wouldn't have been there's if he hadn't come on board.

"With Rasheed coming late and losing quality people," said Brown, "he made our whole team better. I think most people felt when he came here that he was going to be a defensive force, and he was in a lot of ways, but his presence defensively with Ben and Tayshaun gave us unbelievable shot blocking, quickness, unselfish play. There's no way I would be standing up here, or any of us would in this kind of situation, without him."

Said Rasheed: "I just think I added a little bit of defense to his team, but they were already a great ball club. Larry was already a great coach, even before he came to the Pistons. I thank Joe for bringing me here and it worked out for the best."

Billups said he'd kidnap Rasheed's infant daughter to keep him in Detroit. He didn't have to. On July 23 he signed a five-year deal for him $57 million-plus.

"Two weeks after he got here I told him I don't know what's going on with you, but I'm going to have to hold somebody hostage," said Billups. "You've got a new daughter, I'm taking her. She's going to like Detroit because she ain't leaving. I'm keeping her, everybody; the wife, kids. So I don't think he has much of a choice."

MVP Candidate (Non-Player Division): Joe Dumars

He didn't get Executive of the Year this year, but the move he made to get Rasheed put the team over the top and eventually got him a title, his third, two coming as a player.

"I am more relieved now," he said, puffing on a cigar the way Boston coach Red Auerbach used to do during the Celtic dynasty. "There was a lot of pressure, stress and strain. To get it done like this in a short period of time, especially from where we were, is real gratifying. When you are a player, you are young. Your perspective is not there. I am an old man at 41 right now, and I understand it better and appreciate it more not knowing that you'd ever get back again. After you win two championships 15 years ago, you may never know if you'll know what it is like to win one again. It's incredible for me.

"I thought we were a better team than them, plain and simple. I knew they had the two best players in the world, but this is not a tennis match, it is basketball. It is how deep your team is, and we have a deep team. I knew they had two great players, but I also knew we had a better team."

There's that word again: team.

Partying with the Fans

The Palace doors had to open two hours early because 3,000 fans were lingering around the lobby waiting to get in.

Indeed, Michigan and Detroit went from Motown to 'Fro Town as the state celebrated the Pistons' third NBA championship as an estimated one million fans filled Hart Plaza in the morning before packing the Palace late in the afternoon.

Dumars Gives the Crowd Its Due

Joe Dumars sat with a big unlit cigar in his mouth as hundreds of thousands of fans shouted "Bad Boys, Bad Boys." He doesn't drink or smoke.

"I want to thank all you fans," said Dumars. "You guys are definitely the best fans in the world. Larry Brown and his coaching staff came here under a tremendous amount of scrutiny, and you are without a doubt the best coaching staff I've ever been around. These players represented you extremely well and I'm just thinking we're going to try and get back here again next year. We got some free agents here: Rasheed, Memo and Mike James. You guys just let them know you want them back.

"You can forget if you don't get to see what you saw today. Just looking at people's faces today ... it's pretty amazing. People want to feel good about their city. They want to say 'our city is No. 1.' And one of the things that can make a city feel good is their sports team.

"It was a great parade and these people are wonderful. Today was a reminder of how great the fans are here. They keep saying bring the team back. Don't worry, we will."

New Cabinet Post

Gov. Jennifer Granholm, speaking for the 10 million citizens in the state of Michigan, named Ben Wallace Secretary of Defense at Detroit's downtown Hart Plaza.

Who Was the Favorite?

Spicy owner Bill Davidson stunned the crowd with his assessment of his third championship. "Over the past couple of weeks there has been a lot of bullshit going on in this country. Let me be a little more refined and say misconceptions. Let's start with the 8-to-1 odds the Lakers had in beating the Pistons.

"Actually, they were lucky to win one game. Next, we go to our fans in the arena. Absolutely no contest with the L.A. Lakers. Obviously, they expected their team to win easy. Our fans were the greatest in the country and national TV showed it to be the case. No.1, without any question.

"Now to the city of Detroit and you fans today. Once again, a lot of bullshit going on as to how you were going to respond to the victory. You responded in the most magnificent way possible. You've done it in a wonderful, remarkable way. The city of Detroit is the No. 1 city in terms of support to its basketball team."

He toned down his comments at the Palace.

"You are no longer a secret," Davidson told the crowd.

No. 1 Stunner

The Larry O'Brien Trophy was with Ben and Chanda Wallace most of the day, and that's where it belonged. Ben walked into Hart Plaza with it and he walked into the Palace with it.

His Blue Kangol covering the 'Fro, Ben said: "It was exciting for the crowd to come out and support us the way they have. Our work is done.

"Thank y'all for coming out every night rocking that Palace, cheering the way y'all did. I want to thank Joe D. for giving me the opportunity of coming here. He told me he just wasn't bringing me here to be here. He was bringing me here to win a championship. I'd like to thank Coach [Larry] Brown and his staff for allowing me to play basketball. I'm not just a defensive specialist, I'm a basketball player."

Ouch, Rick Carlisle.

21 Years in the Making

Larry Brown won his first NBA title after 21 years on numerous benches across the league.

"My wife met the players when she first got here and told me we had a special group of players, and when she met the wives she said she could tell why they were a special group," said Brown. "I've been a lot of places and coached a lot of teams and had a lot of great coaches work with me. We have the greatest staff of people here. Mr. D., Joe, John [Hammond], Tom [Wilson]. I never worked with a group that worked as hard to get us to where we are.

"In the last two days I've gotten calls from everywhere, and all the people wanted to talk about was how unselfish and hardworking and how these guys wanted to play the right way. Care about one another and try to treat each other the right way, and it's amazing what you can accomplish."

Brown took pictures with policeman and signed shirts.

"It's pretty special, especially in this city," said Brown. "This whole ride this year, we wouldn't be here if it wasn't for this city and this people. I just hope we represent this city the way they want. I love to coach and teach and this is a group that reflects doing things the right way. Let's try this again next year; this is good."

Prince of the Palace

When talking about the championship, quiet Tayshaun Prince also came out of his shell.

"You guys are definitely the best in the country," he said. "You definitely have to thank Joe Dumars. I'd like to thank all 22 teams that had a chance to draft me and didn't do it. That's who I'd like to thank the most. Words can't really describe how I feel right now. It's the best feeling in the world. This is a family. The chemistry around this team has been unbelievable."

Chauncey Billups Has Finally Found a Home

"I don't plan on going anywhere," said Billups. "This is a dream come true for me. I've been through the ringer and I never gave up. God is good. It taught me to move on and taught me to dwell on what's going on and not worry about the past. I believe in going out and just controlling the things I can control.

"We're back, baby, the Bad Boys are back, baby. I wish our arena could hold a million people because I know all of you would be there. We'll be back here next year.

"At the start of the year everybody was talking about who we didn't draft, but all I've got to say is, Carmelo who?"

Let 'Er Rip

"It was crazy," said Richard Hamilton. "Yessir. I love these dudes. The one thing about us, if you get through one of us, there's 11 more you have to get through. We try to work hard and do what we have to do to get a win. This is my home right here.

"We have the best fans in the world and we just try to enjoy it. When Joe traded for me, he said this is going to be your home. He said this is the place where you're going to win a championship."

Quotes from the Rest of the Gang

"I like to thank Joe D. for not bringing me back not just once, but twice," said Lindsey Hunter.

"The next year you are the target," said Chuck Daly. "It's unbelievably difficult."

Mehmet Okur: "You are the best and I feel so special because these guys are the best."

Darvin Ham: "When you played the Bad Boys you knew you were in for a fight every night. I just thank God we were able to bring the trophy back to Detroit."

Elden Campbell: "I really feel blessed now. I want to thank Joe and the owner for the opportunity. I think they kind of wrote me out last year. Thanks to the doctors for the medicine, right, because I'm hurting."

Mike James: "I just want to thank God, my wife and my family."

Corliss Williamson: "We love to give the praise and the glory to the almighty God. We all worked extremely hard to this whole season. We have a great owner and a great coach and Joe did a great job."

A Last Roundup

It was the last time this group would all be together as a team.

Williamson was traded for Derrick Coleman and Amal McCaskill in early August. James wasn't re-signed and went to Milwaukee.

Okur became a rich member of the Utah Jazz. But two days after winning the championship they were all together for one more celebration.